Trip to Hanoi

Trip to Hanoi

SUSAN SONTAG

FARRAR, STRAUS AND GIROUX

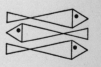

NEW YORK

Trip to Hanoi

THOUGH I HAVE BEEN AND AM PASSIONATELY OPPOSED to the American aggression in Vietnam, I accepted the unexpected invitation to go to Hanoi that came in mid-April with the pretty firm idea that I wouldn't write about the trip upon my return. Being neither a journalist nor a political activist (though a veteran signer of petitions and anti-war demonstrator) nor an Asian specialist, but rather a stubbornly unspecialized writer who has so far been largely unable to incorporate into either novels or essays my evolving radical political convictions and sense of moral dilemma at being a citizen of the American empire, I doubted that my account of such a trip could add anything new to the already eloquent opposition to the war. And contributing to the anti-war polemic seemed to me the only worthwhile reason for an American to be writing about Vietnam now.

Perhaps the difficulty started there, with the lack of a purpose that really justified in my own mind my being invited to North Vietnam. Had I brought some clear intentions about the usefulness (to me or to anyone else) of my visit, I probably would have found it easier to sort out and assimilate what I saw. If occasionally I could have reminded myself that I was a writer and Vietnam was "material," I might have fended off some of the confusions that beset me. As it was, the first days of my stay were profoundly discouraging, with most of my energies going toward trying to keep my gloom within tolerable limits. But now that I'm back, and since returning want after all to write about North Vietnam, I don't regret that early decision. By denying myself a role that could have shielded me from my ignorance and spared me a lot of personal discomfort, I unwittingly assisted what discoveries I eventually did make during the trip.

Of course, it wasn't only this original refusal to envisage the trip as a professional task that opened the way to my confusion. In part, my bewilderment was direct and unavoidable: the honest reflex of being culturally dislocated. Also, I should mention that few Americans who visit Hanoi at this time go alone, the usual practice being, for the convenience of the Vietnamese, to assemble groups of sometimes two, usually three, four, or five people who often don't know each other before the trip. I traveled to North Vietnam as one of three. And I had met neither of the two other Americans in whose company I made the trip—Andrew Kopkind, the journalist, and Robert Greenblatt, a mathematician from Cornell now working full time for the anti-war movement—before our rendezvous in Cambodia in late April. Yet this trip involves unremitting and not wholly voluntary proximity, the kind befitting a romance or a dangerous emergency, lasting without pause for at least a month. (We were invited for two weeks. It took us ten days, because of delays and missed connections, to go from New York via Paris and Phnom Penh to Hanoi, and just under a week to make the return trip.) Naturally, the situation with my companions claimed a sizable part of the attention that, had I traveled alone, would have gone to the Vietnamese: sometimes in the form of an obligation, most often as a pleasure. There was the practical necessity of learning to live amicably and intelligently with two strangers in circumstances of instant intimacy, strangers even if, or perhaps especially since, they were people already known to me by reputation and, in the case of Andy Kopkind, by his writing, which I admired. We were further drawn together by being in what was to all three of us an alien part of the world (neither Bob Greenblatt nor I had ever been to Asia before; Andy Kopkind had made one trip five years ago, visiting Saigon, Bangkok, the Philippines, and Japan), and meeting no one whose native language was English (except a U.S.I.S. official and an American journalist in Laos, where we were stuck for four days on our way "in," and four American college students sponsored by S.D.S. who arrived in Hanoi at the beginning of our second week). All this added together, it seems inevitable that we spent a great deal of time talking—gratefully, often feverishly—to each other.

Still, I don't mean to suggest that these elements of my situation account for the wistfully negative tone of my early impressions of Vietnam. The serious explanation for that I would locate not in the distractions and pressures of being one of an arbitrarily assembled yet inseparable trio in a new land, but in the demands and limitations of the approach to Vietnam I myself was capable of. Made

miserable and angry for four years by knowledge of the
excruciating suffering of the Vietnamese people at the
hands of my government, now actually there and being
plied with gifts and flowers and rhetoric and tea and seem-
ingly exaggerated kindness, I didn't *feel* any more than I
already had ten thousand miles away. But being in Hanoi
was far more mysterious, more puzzling intellectually,
than I expected. I found that I couldn't avoid worrying
and wondering how well I understood the Vietnamese, and
they me and my country.

Yet this problem I posed for myself, frustrating as it
proved, was perhaps the most important and fruitful one,
at least to me. For it was not information (at least in the
ordinary sense) that I'd come to find. Like anyone who
cared about Vietnam in the last years, I already knew a
great deal; and I could not hope to collect more or sig-
nificantly better information in a mere two weeks than was
already available. Ranging from the early reports in *The
New York Times* by Harrison Salisbury of his visit in
December and January of 1965–66 (later expanded into a
book, *Behind the Lines—Hanoi*) and *The Other Side,* the
book written jointly by Staughton Lynd and Tom Hayden,
the first Americans from the anti-war movement to visit
North Vietnam, to the analyses of Philippe Devillers and
Jean Lacouture in the French press, to the recent articles
by Mary McCarthy which I've been reading since my
return to the United States, a multiple account has ac-
cumulated which conveys in vivid detail how Hanoi and
large parts of North Vietnam appear to a sympathetic or
at least reasonably objective outsider looking on. Anyone

who wants to can get information on the achievements of the country since the French left in 1954: the expansion of medical services, the reorganization of education, the creation of a modest industrial base, and the beginnings of diversified agriculture. Even easier to obtain are the facts about the years of merciless bombing by the United States of all the population centers of North Vietnam—with the exception of downtown Hanoi (which has, however, been doused with "anti-personnel" or fragmentation bombs, those that don't harm buildings but only kill people)—and the destruction of virtually all the new schools and hospitals and factories built since 1954, as well as most bridges, theatres, pagodas, and Catholic churches and cathedrals. In my own case, several years of reading and of viewing newsreels had furnished a large portfolio of miscellaneous images of Vietnam: napalmed corpses, live citizens on bicycles, the hamlets of thatched huts, the razed cities like Nam Dinh and Phu Ly, the cylindrical, one-person bomb shelters spaced along the sidewalks of Hanoi, the thick yellow straw hats worn by schoolchildren as protection against fragmentation bombs. (Indelible horrors, pictorial and statistical, supplied by courtesy of television and *The New York Times* and *Life,* without one's even having to bestir oneself to consult the frankly partisan books of Wilfred Burchett or the documentation assembled by the Russell Foundation's International War Crimes Tribunal.) But the confrontation with the originals of these images didn't prove to be a simple experience; actually to see and touch them produced an effect both exhilarating and numbing. Matching concrete reality with mental image was at best a mechanical or merely additive process, while prying new facts from the Vietnamese officials and ordinary citizens I was meeting was a task for which I'm not particularly well equipped. Unless I could effect in myself some change of awareness, of consciousness, it would scarcely matter that I'd actually been to Vietnam. But that was exactly what was so hard, since I had only my own culture-bound, disoriented sensibility for an instrument.

Indeed, the problem was that Vietnam had become so much a fact of my consciousness as an American that I was having enormous difficulty getting it outside my head. The first experience of being there absurdly resembled meeting a favorite movie star, one who for years has played a role in one's fantasy life, and finding the actual person so much smaller, less vivid, less erotically charged, and mainly different. Most convincing were the experiences that were least real, like the evening of our arrival. I was nervous throughout the flight in the small International Control Commission plane that had belatedly taken off from Vientiane; and landing in Hanoi's Gia Lam airport at night several hours later, I was mainly relieved just to be alive and on the ground, and hardly bothered that I knew neither where I was nor whom I was with. Hugging my flowers, I crossed the dark landing area, trying to keep straight the names of the four smiling men from the Peace Committee who had come to meet us. And if our flight and landing had the quality of a hallucination, the rest of that night seemed like one vast back projection, with overvivid extensions and foreshortenings of time, scale,

and movement. First, there were either the few minutes or
the hour spent waiting for our luggage in the bleak airport
building, awkwardly chatting with the Vietnamese. Then,
when we were distributed in three cars and started into
the darkness, there was the rhythm of the ride into Hanoi.
A little way from the airport, the cars lurched down a
bumpy dirt road onto the narrow, shuddering pontoon
bridge over the Red River that has replaced the bombed-
out iron one, and inched across that; but once on the other
side, the cars seemed to go too fast and, entering Hanoi,
passing through dim streets, opened a rude swathe in the
stream of indistinguishable figures on bicycles, until we
halted in front of our hotel. Its name, Thong Nhat, means
Reunification, someone said: a huge building, and indeter-
minate in style. A dozen people were sitting about the
very plain lobby, mostly non-Orientals but at that point
otherwise unidentifiable. After we were taken upstairs and
shown to our large rooms, there was a late supper for us
in a stark, deserted dining room with rows of propeller
fans slowly turning overhead. "Our" Vietnamese waited
for us in the lobby. When we joined them, we asked if,
late as it was, they would mind going out with us for a
walk. So out we went, weak with excitement. Along the
streets, now almost empty of people, we passed clusters
of trucks parked between tents which, they told us, shel-
tered all-night "mobile workshops" or "dispersed factories." We went as far as the Mot Cot pagoda in the Petit
Lac, and lingering there, heard some—to me, barely intel-
ligible—tales of ancient Vietnamese history. Once back in
the hotel lobby, Oanh, evidently the leader of the group

from the Peace Committee, gently urged us to go to bed. People in Hanoi, he explained, rise and eat breakfast very early (since the bombing started, most stores open at 5 A.M. and close a few hours later), and they would be coming by for us at 8 A.M. the next day, which happened to be Buddha's birthday, to take us to a pagoda. I remember reluctantly saying good night to the Vietnamese and to my two companions; in my room, spending a quarter of an hour trying to cope with the high vault of white mosquito netting covering the bed; and finally sinking into a difficult, agitated, but happy sleep.

Of course, North Vietnam was unreal that first night. But it continued to seem unreal, or at least incomprehensible, for days afterwards. To be sure, that initial haunting vision of wartime Hanoi at night was corrected by more mundane daytime experiences. The Thong Nhat Hotel shrank to ordinary size (one could even visualize it in its former incarnation, the Metropole of French colonial days); individuals of varying age and character emerged out of the silent collective traffic of bicyclists and pedestrians; and the Petit Lac and the nearby tree-shaded streets became places of daily resort, where we walked casually, without our guides, whenever it wasn't too hot and one or two or all three of us had a spare hour. Though so far from and so unlike the only cities I knew, those of America and Europe, Hanoi quickly gained an eerie familiarity. Yet when I was honest with myself I had to admit that the place was simply too foreign, that I really understood nothing at all, except at a "distance."

In his brilliant episode in the film *Far from Vietnam,*

Godard reflects (as we hear his voice, we see him sitting behind an idle movie camera) that it would be good if we each made a Vietnam inside ourselves, especially if we cannot actually go there (Godard had wanted to shoot his episode in North Vietnam, but was denied a visa). Godard's point—a variant on Che's maxim that, in order to crack the American hegemony, revolutionaries have the duty to create "two, three, many Vietnams"—had seemed to me exactly right. What I'd been creating and enduring for the last four years was a Vietnam inside my head, under my skin, in the pit of my stomach. But the Vietnam I'd been thinking about for years was scarcely filled out at all. It was really only the mold into which the American seal was cutting. My problem was not to try to feel more inside myself. My problem was that I (luckier than Godard) was now actually in Vietnam for a brief time, yet somehow was unable to make the full intellectual and emotional connections that my political and moral solidarity with Vietnam implied.

The most economical way, I think, of conveying these early difficulties is to transcribe from journal entries I made during the first week after our arrival on the third of May.

MAY 5

The cultural difference is the hardest thing to estimate, to overcome. A difference of manners, style, therefore of substance. (And how much of what I'm struck by is Asian, how much specifically Vietnamese, I am unlikely to find out on my first trip to Asia.) Clearly, they have a different way here of treating the guest, the stranger, the foreigner, not to mention the enemy. Also, I'm convinced, the Vietnamese have a different relation to language. The difference can't just be due to the fact that my sentences, already slowed down and simplified, more often than not have to be mediated by a translator. For even when I'm in conversation with someone who speaks English or French, it seems to me we're both talking baby talk.

To all this add the constraint of being reduced to the status of a child: scheduled, led about, explained to, fussed over, pampered, kept under benign surveillance. Not only a child individually but, even more exasperating, one of a group of children. The four Vietnamese from the Peace Committee who are seeing us around act as our nurses, our teachers. I try to discover the differences between each of them, but can't; and I worry that they don't see what's different or special about me. All too often I catch myself trying to please them, to make a good impression—to get the best mark of the class. I present myself as an intelligent, well-mannered, cooperative, uncomplicated person. So not only do I feel like a rather corrupt child but, being neither a child nor in fact as simple and easy to know as the way I'm coming on would indicate, I feel somewhat of a fraud. (It's no extenuation that this open, legible person is perhaps who I would like to be.)

Maybe, if I'm cheating, with the best intentions, trying to make it easier for them, they're doing the same for us. Is that why, though I know they must be different from each other, I can't get beyond the surface markings? Oanh has the most personal authority, walks and sits with that charming "American" slouch, and sometimes seems moody or distracted. (We've learned that his wife has been ill ever since she was captured and tortured for a year by the French in the early 1950's; and he has several small children.) Hieu alternates between boyishness—he giggles —and the pointed composure of a junior bureaucrat. Phan has the most affable manners; he usually seems out of breath when he talks, which he loves doing; he's also one of the very few plump Vietnamese I've seen. Toan generally looks eager and slightly intimidated, and never speaks unless you ask him a question. But what else? Phan is the oldest, I think. Today we learned, to our great surprise, that Oanh is forty-six. It doesn't help that every Vietnamese (especially the men, who rarely go bald or even gray) looks at least ten years younger than he is.

What makes it especially hard to see people as individuals is that everybody here seems to talk in the same style and to have the same things to say. This impression is reinforced by the exact repetition of the ritual of hospitality at each place we visit. A bare room, a low table, wooden chairs, perhaps a couch. We all shake hands, then sit around the table, which holds several plates of overripe green bananas, Vietnamese cigarettes, damp cookies, a dish of paper-wrapped candies made in China, cups for tea. We are introduced. They tell us their names. We shake hands again. Pause. The spokesman of their group, wherever we are visiting (a factory, a school, a government ministry, a museum), gazes at us benignly, smiles. *"Cac ban* . . . " ("Friends . . . ") He has started his speech of welcome. Someone comes through a curtain and begins serving tea.

MAY 6

Of course, I'm not sorry to have come. Being in Hanoi is at the very least a duty, for me an important act of personal and political affirmation. What I'm not yet reconciled to is that it's also a piece of political theatre. They are playing their roles, we (I) must play ours (mine). The heaviness of it all comes from the fact that the script is written entirely by them; and they're directing the play, too. Though this is how it has to be—it's their country, their life-and-death struggle, while we are volunteers, extras, figurants who retain the option of getting off the stage and sitting safely in the audience—it makes my acts here appear to me largely dutiful, and the whole performance a little sad.

We have a role: American friends of the Vietnamese struggle. (About forty Americans in some way connected with the anti-war movement in the States have made this trip before us.) The trip to Hanoi is a kind of reward or patronage. We are being given a treat, being thanked for our unsolicited efforts; and then we are to return home with a reinforced sense of solidarity, to continue our separate ways of opposing the current American policy.

There is, of course, an exquisite politeness in this corporate identity. We are not asked, separately or collectively, to say why we merit this trip. Our being recommended (by Americans who were invited earlier and retain the confidence of the Vietnamese) and our willingness to come (all this way, at our own expense, and facing the risk of prosecution when we return to the States) seem to put Bob's, Andy's, and my efforts on the same level. Nobody here poses questions about what we specifically do for the anti-war movement, or asks us to justify the quality of our activities; it seems to be assumed that we each do what we can. Though our Vietnamese hosts evidently know we are not Communists, and indeed seem to have no illusions about the American Communist Party—"We know our Communist friends in the United States are not in great number," a government official remarked dryly—nobody inquires into our political beliefs. We are *cac ban* all.

Everybody says, "We know the American people are our friends. Only the present American government is our enemy." A journalist we met commended our efforts to "safeguard the freedom and prestige of the United States." Though I honor the nobility of this attitude, I'm exasperated by their naïveté. Do they really believe what they're saying? Don't they understand anything about America? Part of me can't help regarding them as children—beautiful, patient, heroic, martyred, stubborn children. And I know that I'm not a child, though the theatre of this visit requires that I play the role of one. The same shy, tender smile appears on the face of the soldier we pass in the park, the elderly Buddhist scholar, and the waitress in the hotel dining room as on the faces of the children lined up to greet us at the evacuated primary school we visited today just outside Hanoi; and we're smiling at them like that, too. We get little presents and souvenirs wherever we

go, and at the end of each visit Bob distributes a handful
of anti-war buttons (how lucky that he thought to bring a
bagful of them). The most impressive of his random
collection are the jumbo blue and white buttons from last
October's March on the Pentagon, which we save for
special occasions. How could we not be moved at the moment we are pinning on their tiny red and gold badges
while they are adorning themselves with our big anti-war
buttons? How could we not also be in bad faith?

The root of my bad faith: that I long for the three-
dimensional, textured, "adult" world in which I live in
America—even as I go about my (their) business in this
two-dimensional world of the ethical fairy tale where I am
paying a visit, and in which I do believe.

Part of the role (theirs and mine) is the stylizing of
language: speaking mostly in simple declarative sentences,
making all discourse either expository or interrogative.
Everything is on one level here. All the words belong to
the same vocabulary: struggle, bombings, friend, aggres-
sor, imperialist, patriot, victory, brother, freedom, unity,
peace. Though my strong impulse is to resist their flatten-
ing out of language, I've realized that I must talk this
way—with moderation—if I'm to say anything that's useful to them. That even includes using the more loaded
local epithets like "the puppet troops" (for the forces of
the Saigon government) and "the American movement"
(they mean *us!*). Luckily, I'm already comfortable with
some of the key words. Within the last year, back in the
States, I had started saying "the Front" (instead of Viet
Cong) and "black people" (instead of Negroes) and

"liberated zones" (for territory controlled by the National Liberation Front). But I'm far from getting it right, from their point of view. I notice that when I say "Marxism," it's usually rendered by our translator as "Marxism-Leninism." And while they may speak of "the socialist camp," it's hardly possible for me to say anything other than "Communist countries."

It's not that I judge their words to be false. For once, I think, the political and moral reality is as simple as the Communist rhetoric would have it. The French *were* "the French colonialists"; the Americans *are* "imperialist aggressors"; the Thieu-Ky regime *is* a "puppet government." Then what finicky private standard or bad vibrations make me balk? Is it just the old conviction of the inadequacy of that language, to which I was first introduced during my precociously political childhood when I read *PM* and Corliss Lamont and the Webbs on Russia, and later, by the time I was a junior at North Hollywood High School, worked in the Wallace campaign and attended screenings of Eisenstein films at the American-Soviet Friendship Society? But surely neither the philistine fraud of the American CP nor the special pathos of fellow-traveling in the 1940's is relevant here: North Vietnam, spring 1968. Yet how difficult it is, once words have been betrayed, to take them seriously again. Only within the last two years (and that very much because of the impact of the Vietnam war) have I been able to pronounce the words "capitalism" and "imperialism" again. For more than fifteen years, though capitalism and imperialism hardly ceased to be facts in the world, the words themselves had seemed to me simply unusable, dead, dishonest (because a tool in the hands of dishonest people). A great deal is involved in these recent linguistic decisions: a new connection with my historical memory, my aesthetic sensibility, my very idea of the future. That I've begun to use some elements of Marxist or neo-Marxist language again seems almost a miracle, an unexpected remission of historical muteness, a new chance to address problems that I'd renounced ever understanding.

Still, when I hear these tag words here, spoken by the Vietnamese, I can't help experiencing them as elements of an *official* language, and they become again an alien way of talking. I'm not referring now to the truth of this language (the realities that the words point to), which I do acknowledge, but to the context and range of sensibility it presupposes. What's painfully exposed for me, by the way the Vietnamese talk, is the gap between ethics and aesthetics. As far as I can tell, the Vietnamese possess—even within the terribly austere and materially deprived existence they are forced to lead now—a lively, even passionate aesthetic sense. More than once, for instance, people have quite unaffectedly expressed their indignation and sadness at the disfigurement of the *beauty* of the Vietnamese countryside by the American bombing. Someone even commented on the "many beautiful names," like Cedar Falls and Junction City, that the Americans have given their "savage operations in the south." But the leading way of thinking and speaking in Vietnam is unreservedly moralistic. (I suspect this is quite natural to the Vietnamese, a cultural trait that precedes any grafting on of the moralizing framework of Communist language.)

And perhaps it's the general tendency of aesthetic consciousness, when developed, to make judgments more
complex and more highly qualified, while it's in the very
nature of moral consciousness to be simplifying, even
simplistic, and to sound—in translation at least—stiff and
old-fashioned. There's a committee here (someone had
left a piece of stationery in the hotel lobby) for maintaining contact with South Vietnamese intellectuals, called
"Committee of Struggle Against U.S. Imperialists and
Henchmen's Persecution of Intellectuals in South Vietnam." Henchmen! But aren't they? In today's Vietnam
News Agency bulletin the American soldiers are called
"cruel thugs." Although again the quaintness of phrase
makes me smile, that is just what they are—from the
vantage point of helpless peasants being napalmed by
swooping diving metal birds. Still, quite apart from the
quaintness of particular words, such language does make
me uncomfortable. Whether because I am laggard or
maybe just dissociated, I both assent to the unreserved
moral judgment and shy away from it, too. I believe they
are right. At the same time, nothing here can make me
forget that events are much more complicated than the
Vietnamese represent them. But exactly what complexities
would I have them acknowledge? Isn't it enough that their
struggle is, objectively, just? Can they ever afford subtle-
ties when they need to mobilize every bit of energy to
continue standing up to the American Goliath? . . .
Whatever I conclude, it seems to me I end up patronizing
them.

Perhaps all I'm expressing is the difference between

being an actor (them) and being a spectator (me). But that's a big difference, and I don't see how I can bridge it. My sense of solidarity with the Vietnamese, however genuine and felt, is a moral abstraction developed (and meant to be lived out) at a great distance from them. Since my arrival in Hanoi, I must maintain that sense of solidarity alongside new unexpected feelings which indicate that, unhappily, it will always remain a moral abstraction. For me—a spectator?—it's monochromatic here, and I feel oppressed by that.

MAY 7

Now, I think, I really understand—for the first time—the difference between history and psychology. It's the world of psychology that I miss. (What I meant yesterday by the "adult" world.) They live exclusively in the world of history.

And not only in history, but in a monothematic history that people allude to in more or less the same terms wherever we go. Today we got it in full, during a long guided tour of the Historical Museum: four thousand years of continuous history, more than two thousand years of being overrun by foreign aggressors. The first successful Vietnamese uprising against foreign rule, in A.D. 40, was led by two women generals, the Trung sisters. That was over a thousand years before Joan of Arc, our woman guide at the museum added, as if to indicate we hadn't registered the proper surprise at the idea of a woman general. And you also have two of them, I joked back. She smiled slightly, then went on: "The tradition of the two sisters remains until now. In the present struggle many ladies have shown themselves worthwhile." No pleasantry, that. Oanh, who we've learned is one of the leading composers in North Vietnam, has written a song about the two sisters, and many temples in Hanoi and nearby are dedicated to them. . . . As the Vietnamese understand their history, it consists essentially of one scenario, which has been played out over and over again. Particular historical identities dissolve into instructive equivalences. The Americans = the French (who first entered Vietnam in 1787 with missionaries, and officially invaded the country in 1858) = the Japanese (in World War II) = the "Northern feudalists" (our guide's usual way of referring to the millennia of invading Chinese, I suppose out of politeness to the nominal ally of today). The general who repelled the Chinese invasion of 1075–76, Ly Thuong Kiet, was a poet as well and used his poems to rouse the Vietnamese people to take up arms—just like Ho Chi Minh, the guide pointed out. She told us the generals who defended the country against three invasions by "the Mongols" (another euphemism for the Chinese?) in the thirteenth century—in 1257, 1284–85, and 1287–88— originated the basic techniques of guerrilla warfare that General Giap successfully employed against the French between 1946 and 1954 and now uses against the Americans. In one room, examining a terrain map of the battle site, we learned that the turning point in a struggle against an invasion by two hundred thousand Manchu dynasty troops in 1789 was a surprise Tet offensive. As she relates, with the aid of maps and dioramas, the great sea battles

on the Bach Dang River in 938 and 1288 which successfully terminated other wars of resistance, I detect unmis-
takable parallels to the strategies used at Dien Bien Phu.
(The other night we saw an hour film on the Dien Bien
Phu campaign, part original footage and part reconstruc-
tion. Today, by the way, is the anniversary of that victory,
though I've seen no signs in Hanoi of any festivities.)

My first reaction to the didactically positive way the
Vietnamese have of recounting their history is to find it
simple-minded ("childish" again). I have to remind myself that historical understanding can have other purposes
than the ones I take for granted: objectivity and completeness. This is history for use—for survival, to be precise—
and it is an entirely *felt* history, not the preserve of
detached intellectual concern. The past continues in the
form of the present, and the present extends backward in
time. I see that there's nothing arbitrary or merely quaint
(as I'd thought) in the standard epithet for Americans
which I've seen on billboards and wall posters: *giac My
xan luoc,* "pirate American aggressors." The very first foreign invaders were pirates. So the Chinese, the French, the
Japanese, now the Americans, and anybody else who in-
vades Vietnam will always be pirates, too.

Even more than the Jews, the Vietnamese seem to suffer
from an appalling lack of variety in their collective existence. History is one long martyrdom: in the case of
Vietnam, the chain of episodes of victimization at the
hands of great powers. And one of their proudest boasts is
that people here have succeeded in retaining "Vietnamese
characteristics, though we live close to the Chinese super-

power and were under complete French domination for eighty years," in the words of our guide today. Perhaps only a martyr people, one which has managed to survive against crushing odds, develops so acute and personal a historical concern. And this extraordinarily vivid sense of history—of living simultaneously in the past, the present, and the future—must be one of the great sources of Vietnamese strength.

But the decision to survive at all costs in suffering obviously imposes its own aesthetic, its own peculiar and (to people not consciously driven by the imperative of survival) maddening sensibility. The Vietnamese historical sense, being, above all, a sense of the sameness of history, is reflected, naturally, in the sameness of what they say—what they feel we ought to listen to. I've become aware here of how greatly prized, and taken for granted, the value of *variety* is in Western culture. In Vietnam, apparently, something doesn't become less valuable or useful because it has been done (or said) before. On the contrary, repetition confers value on something. It is a positive moral style. Hence, the capsule summaries of Vietnamese history we get from most people we visit, almost as much a part of the ritual as the tea and green bananas and expressions of friendship for the American people whom we're supposed to represent.

But further, these speeches of historical recital that we hear almost daily are just one symptom of the general predilection of the Vietnamese for putting all information into a historical narrative. I've noticed that when we're discussing or asking questions about the country today, each account given to us is formulated around a pivotal date: usually either August 1945 (victory of the Vietnamese revolution, the founding of the state by Ho Chi Minh) or 1954 (expulsion of the French colonialists) or 1965 (beginning of "the escalation," as they call the American bombing). Everything is either before or after something else.

Their framework is chronological. Mine is both chronological and geographical. I am continually reaching toward cross-cultural comparisons, and these are the context of most of my questions. But because they don't share this context, they seem mildly puzzled by many things I ask. How hard it was yesterday, for instance, to get the affable, French-educated Minister of Higher Education, Professor Ta Quang Buu, to explore the differences between the French lycée curriculum used until 1954 and the program the Vietnamese have devised to replace it. Though he heard my question, for a while he simply didn't see the point of it. All he wanted was to outline the Vietnamese system (kindergarten plus ten grades), report how few schools of any kind existed before 1954 and how many have been opened since (except for a good medical school inherited from the French, almost all university-level facilities have had to be developed from scratch), cite figures on rising literacy, tell how increasing numbers of teachers have been trained and young people given access to higher education and older people enrolled in adult-education courses since that date. The same thing happened when we talked to the Minister of Health, Dr. Pham Ngoc Thach, in his office in Hanoi, and when we met the young doctor of the tiny hamlet of Vy Ban in Hoa Binh province. After explaining that most of the Vietnamese population had no medical services of any kind under the French, they were eager to tell us how many hospitals and infirmaries have been built and how many doctors have been trained and to describe the programs undertaken since 1954 that have brought malaria under control and virtually eliminated opium addiction, but were quite taken aback when we wanted to know whether Vietnamese medicine was entirely Western in orientation or whether, as we suspected, Western techniques were mixed with Chinese methods such as herbal medicines and acupuncture. They must find us dilettantish, and may even regard such questions as a means of refusing full emotional solidarity with the unity and urgency of their struggle. Perhaps. It's still true that since Andy, Bob, and I don't share a history with the Vietnamese the historical view does narrow our understanding. To gain insight into what the Vietnamese are trying to build we must relate what they tell us to knowledge and perspectives we already have. But what we know, of course, is just what they don't know. And so most of our questions are a kind of rudeness, to which they respond with unfailing courtesy and patience, but sometimes obtusely.

MAY 8

Judging from these first days, I think it's hopeless. There is a barrier I can't cross. I'm overcome by how exotic the Vietnamese are—impossible for us to understand them, clearly impossible for them to understand us. No, I'm hedging here. The truth is: I feel I *can* in fact understand them (if not relate to them, except on their simplistic terms). But it seems to me that while my consciousness does include theirs, or could, theirs could never include mine. They may be nobler, more heroic, more generous than I am, but I have more on my mind than they do—probably just what precludes my ever being that virtuous. Despite my admiration for the Vietnamese and my shame over the deeds of my country, I still feel like someone from a "big" culture visiting a "little" culture. My consciousness, reared in that "big" culture, is a creature with many organs, accustomed to being fed by a stream of cultural goods, and infected by irony. While I don't think I'm lacking in moral seriousness, I shrink from having my seriousness ironed out; I know I'd feel reduced if there were no place for its contradictions and paradoxes, not to mention its diversions and distractions. Thus, the gluttonous habits of my consciousness prevent me from being at home with what I most admire, and—for all my raging against America—firmly unite me to what I condemn. "American friend" indeed!

Of course, I *could* live in Vietnam, or an ethical society like this one—but not without the loss of a big part of myself. Though I believe incorporation into such a society will greatly improve the lives of most people in the world (and therefore support the advent of such societies), I imagine it will in many ways impoverish mine. I live in an unethical society that coarsens the sensibilities and thwarts the capacities for goodness of most people but makes available for minority consumption an astonishing array of intellectual and aesthetic pleasures. Those who don't enjoy (in both senses) my pleasures have every right, from their side, to regard my consciousness as spoiled, corrupt, decadent. I, from my side, can't deny the immense richness of these pleasures, or my addiction to them. What came to mind this afternoon was the sentence of Talleyrand that Bertolucci used as the motto of his sad, beautiful film: "He who has not lived before the revolution has never known the sweetness of life." I told Andy, who knows the film, what I'd been thinking, and he confessed to similar feelings. We were walking alone in a quarter of Hanoi far from the hotel and, like truants, began talking—nostalgically?—about San Francisco rock groups and *The New York Review of Books*.

Does all this mental appetitiveness and lust for variety disqualify me from entering, at least partially, into the singular reality of North Vietnam? I suspect it does, that it already has, as indicated by my baffled, frustrated reactions to the Vietnamese so far. Maybe I'm only fit to share a people's revolutionary aspirations at a comfortable distance from them and their struggle—one more volunteer in the armchair army of bourgeois intellectuals with radical sympathies in the head. Before I give up, though, I must make sure I've read these feelings correctly. My impulse is to follow the old, severe rule: if you can't put your life where your head (heart) is, then what you think (feel) is a fraud. But it's premature to talk of fraud and hypocrisy. If the test is whether I can put my life (even imaginatively) in Vietnam, the time to take it isn't now but when I have a somewhat less meager grasp of the country.

Even if I fail the test of being able to identify myself with the Vietnamese, what have I actually proven? Perhaps I haven't experienced the constraints, real or imaginary, of ethical—or revolutionary—societies in general, only of this one. Maybe I'm only saying I find something uncongenial about North Vietnam. . . . And yet I do like the Vietnamese, respond to them, feel good with them, sometimes really happy here. Doesn't it all come down to the absurd complaint—the complaint of a real child, me— that people here aren't making it easier for me to perceive them, the wish that the Vietnamese "show" themselves to me clearly so that I can't find them opaque, simple-minded, naïve? Now I'm back where I started. The sense of the barrier between them and me. My not understanding them, their not understanding me. No judgments now (at least none I really believe).

MAY 9

How odd to feel estranged from Vietnam here, when Vietnam has been present in my thoughts every day in America. But if the Vietnam I've carried around like a wound in my heart and mind is not invalidated by what I see in Hanoi, it doesn't seem particularly related to this place at this time either. Having arrived after March 31, we are not under bombardment, though along with every-one else in Hanoi we take shelter at least once a day when the American reconnaissance planes come over. Where civilians are being slaughtered, villages burned, and crops

poisoned, we aren't permitted to go. (Not for reasons of
military security, since earlier American visitors were taken
to areas under bombardment, but out of concern for our
safety: where there's American bombing now, it goes on
almost round the clock. The average daily tonnage of
bombs being dropped on North Vietnam since March 31,
though confined to the area below the 19th parallel, *ex-
ceeds* the daily average unloaded on the whole country
before the "limited bombing pause.") We see only a
handsome, evenly impoverished, clean Asian city; we see
charming, dignified people living amid bleak material
scarcity and the most rigorous demands on their energies
and patience. The leveled towns and villages in the countryside to which we drive on short trips already constitute
a tableau from the past, a thoroughly *accepted* environment in which people go on functioning, working toward
their victory, making their revolution. I wasn't prepared
for all this calm. Thinking about Vietnam in America, it
seems natural to dwell on destruction and suffering. But
not here. In Vietnam, there is also a peaceful, fiercely in-
dustrious present with which a visitor must be connected;
and I'm not. I want their victory. But I don't understand
their revolution.

It's all around me, of course, but I feel I'm in a glass
box. We're supposed to be learning about it through the
"activities" Oanh & Co. have set up in consultation with us
since our arrival. In principle, we wanted to see anything
and everything, and that's what's happening—though individual interests are swiftly catered to. (It was at my
request that we spent an afternoon watching a movie

being shot at the principal film studio in Hanoi; because Bob wanted to meet some mathematicians, a meeting with six math professors from the University of Hanoi was arranged, to which we all ended up going.) We are truly seeing and doing a great deal: at least one visit or meeting is planned for every morning and afternoon, and often in the evening as well, though we have an hour and a half each for lunch and dinner and are encouraged to rest after lunch until three o'clock, when the worst heat of the day is over. In other words, we're in the hands of skilled bureaucrats specializing in relations with foreigners. (Yes, even Oanh—whom I like more and more. Especially he.) All right, I see the inevitability of that. Who else could possibly take charge of us? But even within that framework, shouldn't we be able to go beyond it? I don't think I can. I'm obsessed by the protocol of our situation, which leaves me unable to believe I'm seeing a genuine sample of what this country is like. That suggests the trip isn't going to teach me something usable about revolutionary societies, as I'd assumed it would—unless I count getting so shaken up, as I was yesterday, that I question my right to profess a radical politics at all.

But perhaps there isn't much an American radical *can* learn from the Vietnamese revolution, because the Vietnamese themselves are too alien, in contrast to the considerable amount I think one can learn from the Cuban revolution, because—especially from this perspective—the Cubans are pretty much like us. Though it's probably an error, I can't help comparing the Vietnamese with the Cuban revolution: that is, my experience of it during a three-month stay in Cuba in 1960, plus accounts of how it has developed from friends who've visited more recently. (I probably won't understand anything here until I put Cuba out of my mind. But I can't ignore an experience that seems to me comparable to this one which I felt I did understand and do have imaginative access to.) And almost all my comparisons turn out favorable to the Cubans, unfavorable to the Vietnamese—by the standard of what's useful, instructive, imitable, relevant to American radicalism.

Take, for instance, the populist manners of the Cuban revolution. The Cubans, as I remember well, are informal, impulsive, easily intimate, and manic, even marathon talkers. These may not always be virtues, but they seem so in the context of a successful, entrenched revolutionary society. In Vietnam, everything seems formal, measured, controlled, planned. I long for someone to be indiscreet here. To talk about his personal life, his emotions. To be carried away by "feeling." Instead, everyone is exquisitely polite, yet somehow bland. It fits with the impression Vietnam gives of being an almost sexless culture, from all that I've observed, and from the evidence of the three movies I've seen so far in Hanoi this week and the novel I read last night in English translation. (Hieu confirmed, when I asked him, that there is no kissing in Vietnamese plays and films; obviously there's none in the streets or parks. I haven't seen people touching each other even in a casual way.) As Cuba has proved, a country doesn't have to adopt the puritan style when it goes Communist. And, probably, the Vietnamese attitudes toward sex and the expression of private feeling formed part of this culture long before the advent of revolutionary Marxist idealism. Nevertheless, they do discomfort a Western neo-radical like myself for whom revolution means not only creating political and economic justice but releasing and validating personal (as well as social) energies of all kinds, including erotic ones. And this *is* what revolution has meant in Cuba—despite waves of interference mainly by old-style orthodox Communist bureaucrats, who have been contested by Fidel precisely on this point.

I can't help contrasting the casual egalitarianism I observed among Cubans, whatever their rank or degree of responsibility, with the strongly hierarchical features of this society. No one is in the least servile here, but people know their place. While the deference I notice given to some by others is always graceful, there is clearly the feeling that certain people are more important or valuable than others and deserve a bigger share of the pitifully few comforts available. Hence, the store to which we were taken the third day to get tire sandals and have us each fitted for a pair of Vietnamese trousers. Hieu and Phan told us, with an almost proprietary pride, that this was a special store, reserved for foreigners (diplomatic personnel, guests) and important government people. I thought they should recognize that the existence of such facilities is "un-Communist." But maybe I'm showing here how "American" I am.

I'm troubled, too, by the meals at the Thong Nhat. While every lunch and dinner consists of several delicious meat and fish courses (we're eating only Vietnamese food) and whenever we eat everything in one of the large serving bowls a waitress instantly appears to put another one on our table, ninety-nine percent of the Vietnamese will have rice and bean curd for dinner tonight and are lucky to eat meat or fish once a month. Of course I haven't said anything. They'd probably be mystified, even insulted, if I suggested that we shouldn't be eating so much more than the average citizen's rations. It's well known that lavish and (what would be to us) self-sacrificing hospitality to guests is a staple of Oriental culture. Do I really expect them to violate their own sense of decorum? Still, it bothers me. . . . It also exasperates me that we're driven even very short distances; the Peace Committee has rented two cars, in fact—Volgas—that wait with their drivers in front of the hotel whenever we're due to go anywhere. The office of the NLF delegation in Hanoi, which we visited the other day, was all of two blocks from the hotel. And some of our other destinations proved to be no more than fifteen or twenty blocks away. Why don't they let us walk, as Bob, Andy, and I have agreed among ourselves we'd feel more comfortable doing? Do they have a rule: only the best for the guests? But that kind of politeness, it seems to me, could well be abolished in a Communist society. Or must we go by car because they think we're weak, effete foreigners (Westerners? Americans?) who also need to be reminded to get out of the sun? It disquiets me to think the Vietnamese might regard walking as beneath our dignity (as official guests, celebrities, or something). Whatever their reason, there's no budging them on this. We roll through the crowded streets in our big ugly black cars—the chauffeurs blasting away on their horns to make people on foot and on bicycles watch out, give way. . . . Best, of course, would be if they would lend us, or let us rent, bicycles. But though we've dropped hints to Oanh more than once, it's clear they don't or won't take the request seriously. When we broach it, are they at least amused? Or do they just think we're being silly or impolite or dumb?

All I seem to have figured out about this place is that it's a very complex self that an American brings to Hanoi. At least this American! I sometimes have the miserable feeling that my being here (I won't speak for Andy and Bob) is a big waste of our Vietnamese hosts' time. Oanh should be spending these days writing music. Phan could reread Molière (he taught literature before he started working full-time for the Peace Committee) or visit his teenage daughters, who have been evacuated to the countryside. Hieu, whose profession turns out to be journalism, could be usefully composing articles in the dreadful prose of the North Vietnamese press. Only Toan, who apparently has some clerical job, might lose out; tagging along with the three others to entertain and keep busy the overgrown obtuse foreign guests is probably more amusing than that. What do the Vietnamese imagine is happening to us here? Do they grasp when we understand and when we don't? I'm thinking particularly of Oanh, who is obviously very shrewd and has traveled a lot in Europe, but also of all the smiling people who talk to us, flatter us ("We know your struggle is hard," someone said today), explain things to us. I fear they don't know the difference. They are simply too generous, too credulous.

But I'm also drawn to that kindly credulity. I like how people stare, often gape at us wherever we go in Hanoi. I feel they are enjoying us, that it's a pleasant experience for them to see us. I asked Oanh today if he thought people in the streets realized that we are Americans. He said that most wouldn't. Then who do they think we are, I asked. Probably Russians, was his answer; and indeed, several people have called out *tovarich* and some other Russian word at us. Most people, though, don't say anything in our direction. They stare calmly, point, then discuss us with their neighbors. Hieu says the comment most frequently made about us when we stroll or go to the movies is— delivered with good-natured amazement—how tall we are.

I go out for walks more often by myself now, whenever it's not too hot—trying to relate to the looks people give me, enjoying the ambiguities of my identity, protected by the fact that I don't speak Vietnamese and can only look back and smile. I'm no longer even surprised, as I first was, at how comfortable I am walking alone, even when I get lost in obscure neighborhoods far from the hotel. Though I'm aware of the possibility of an unpleasant incident occurring when I'm in another part of the city, unable to explain who I am or even read signs, I still feel entirely safe. There must be very few foreigners in Hanoi —except within a few blocks of the Thong Nhat, I've seen no one on the streets who isn't Vietnamese; yet here I walk unescorted among these people as if I had a perfect right to be prowling around Hanoi and to expect them all, down to the last old man squatting by the curb selling wooden flutes, to understand that and to ignore me in their amiable way. The impression of civility and lack of violence Hanoi gives is astounding, not just in comparison with any big American city but with Phnom Penh and Vientiane as well. People here are animated, plainly gregarious, but notably unquarrelsome among themselves. Even when the streets are most crowded, there's scarcely any strident noise. Though I see many small but not too well nourished children and babies, I've yet to hear one cry.

Perhaps I feel so secure because I don't take the Vietnamese altogether seriously as "real people," according to the grim view popular where I come from that "real people" are dangerous, volatile; one is never altogether safe with them. I hope it's not that. I know I wouldn't prefer the Vietnamese to be mean or ill-tempered. But as much as I love the deep, sweet silence of Hanoi, I do miss among the Vietnamese a certain element of abrasiveness, a bigger—it doesn't have to be louder—range in their feelings.

For instance, it seems to me a defect that the North Vietnamese aren't good enough haters. How else to explain the odd fact that they actually appear to be quite fond of America? One of the recurrent themes of Dr. Thach's conversation with us was his fervent admiration for America's eminence in technology and science. (This from a cabinet minister of the country being ravaged by the cruelly perfect weapons produced by that very science and technology.) And I suspect that the extent to which the Vietnamese are so interested in and well informed about American politics—as I learned answering some questions put to me in the last days about the Nebraska primary, about Lindsay's influence in Harlem, and about American student radicalism—isn't mere expediency, part of the policy of knowing your enemy, but springs from just plain fascination with the United States. The government and professional people here who have radios listen regularly to the Voice of America and, to be sure, chuckle away at the American version of the war: this week, it's the VOA's denial that any serious military engagements are taking place in Saigon. But at the same time they seem quite respectful of American political processes and even a little sympathetic to the problems America faces as the leading world power. Poets read us verses about "your Walt Whitman" and "your Edgar Allan Poe." At the Writers Union tonight someone asked me if I knew Arthur Miller and flushed with shy pleasure when I said I did and could pass on to him the copy of the Vietnamese translation of *Death of a Salesman* I'd just been shown. "Tell us about your Norman Mailer," a young novelist asked me, and then apologized because Mailer hasn't yet been translated into Vietnamese. And they all wanted to know what kind of books I write, and made me promise to send them copies when I got back to the States. "We are very interested in American literature," someone repeated. Few translations of fiction are being published in Hanoi now, but one of the few this year was an anthology of American short stories: Mark Twain, Jack London, Hemingway,

Dorothy Parker, plus some of the "progressive" writers from the 1930's favored in Eastern Europe. When I mentioned that Americans didn't consider Howard Fast and Albert Maltz in the same class as most others in the collection, one Vietnamese writer assured me they knew that. The trouble was that they actually had very few books—their main library, at the University of Hanoi, was bombed—and most of the volumes of American literature in Hanoi are the choices, and editions, of the Foreign Languages Press in Moscow. "In socialist countries with whom we have normal relations, we can't find modern American writers," he added with a laugh. Another writer who was listening to our conversation grinned.

Of course, I'm delighted to learn that some Vietnamese are not unaware that belonging to the "socialist camp" has its disadvantages—among them, cultural isolation and intellectual provincialism. But it's also sad to think of them carrying the burden of that awareness as well, when they're so acutely conscious of Vietnam as an isolated, provincial country in its own right. Doctors, writers, academics we've talked to speak of feeling desperately cut off. As one professor said, after describing the growth of the science faculties since 1954: "But we still fail to grasp the main tendencies of work going on in the rest of the world. The material we receive is late and not adequate." For all their pride in the progress made since the French were expelled, people often mention to us, apologetically, what a "backward" country Vietnam still is. And then I realize how aware they are that we come from the world's

most "advanced" country; their respect for the United
States is there, whether voiced or not.

It's at these moments that I also feel like the visitor
from America, though in another way. It must be because
I'm so American after all, too profoundly a citizen of the
nation that thinks itself the greatest in everything, that I
feel actually embarrassed by the modest (if proud) self-
affirmation of citizens of a small, weak nation. Their
cordial interest in America is so evidently sincere that it
would be boorish not to respond to it. Yet somehow it
chills me, for it seems a little indecent. I'm aware now
how their unexpectedly complex, yet ingenuous, relation
to the United States overlays every situation between individual Vietnamese and Bob, Andy, and me. But I don't
have the insight or the moral authority to strip us down to
our "real" situation, beyond pathos. My political sympathies being what they are, perhaps there's no way for me
or someone like me to be here except in some stereotyped
capacity (as an "American friend"), no way to avoid
being either self-effacing or passive or sentimental or
patronizing—just as there's no way for Americans, myself
included, not to measure a good six inches taller than the
average Vietnamese.

There are pages more of the same in the first half of the
journal I kept during my stay, interspersed with pages and
pages of detailed notes on each of our visits and encoun-
ters. The strictly reportorial body of my journal, full of
factual information and physical descriptions and summaries of conversations, conveys an attitude of intense,

uncomplicatedly attentive concentration. But the subjective interludes, which I have partly transcribed, convey something else—the callowness and stinginess of my response.

It wasn't that I'd expected to feel at ease in North Vietnam, or to find the Vietnamese as a people exactly like Europeans and Americans. But neither had I expected to be so baffled, so mistrustful of my experiences there—and unable to subdue the backlash of my ignorance. My understanding of the country was limited to Vietnam's election as the target of what's most ugly in America: the principle of "will," the self-righteous taste for violence, the insensate prestige of technological solutions to human problems. I had some knowledge of the style of American will, from living at various times in the Southwest, in California, in the Midwest, in New England, and in recent years in New York, and from observing its impact on Western Europe during the last decade. What I didn't understand, hadn't even a clue to, was the nature of Vietnamese will—its styles, its range, its nuances. Breton has distinguished two forms of the will in authentic revolutionary struggle: "revolutionary patience" and "the cry." But these can't be confronted without grasping something of the specific quality of a people—just what I was finding so difficult in North Vietnam. Whether I concluded that my limitations, or theirs, were being exposed by my inability to have a satisfactory contact with the Vietnamese, the impasse was the same. By around the fifth day, as the extracts from my journal indicate, I was ready to give up—on myself, which meant on the Vietnamese as well.

And then, suddenly, my experience started changing. The psychic cramp with which I was afflicted in the early part of my stay began to ease and the Vietnamese as real people, and North Vietnam as a real place, came into view.

The first sign was that I became more comfortable in talking to people: not only to Oanh, our chief guide—I talked to him more than to any other Vietnamese during my stay—but also to a militia girl or factory worker or schoolteacher or doctor or village leader whom we'd spend an hour with and never see again. I became less preoccupied with the constrictions of their language (a great deal of which I knew must be put down to that "abstractness" or "vagueness" of speech remarked on by Western visitors to every Oriental country) and with the reduction of my own resources of expression, and more sensitive to distinctions in the way the Vietnamese talked. For a start, I could distinguish between a propagandistic level of language (which still may convey the truth, but nevertheless sounds oppressive and wrong) and a merely simple kind of language. I learned, too, to pay more rather than less attention to whatever was constantly reiterated, and discovered the standard words and phrases to be richer than I'd thought.

Take, for instance, the notion of respect. "We respect your Norman Morrison" was a phrase often used in the ceremonial speeches of greeting made to us at each of our visits in Hanoi and in the countryside. We learned that

Oanh had written a popular "Song to Emily"—Norman Morrison's youngest daughter, whom he took along with him when he went to immolate himself in front of the Pentagon. At the Writers Union, someone chanted for us a beautiful poem (which I'd read beforehand in English and French translation) called "The Flame of Morrison." Truck drivers taking supplies along the perilous route down to the 17th parallel are likely to have a picture of Norman Morrison pasted on their sun visors, perhaps alongside a photograph of Nguyen Van Troi, the Saigonese youth who was executed several years ago for plotting to assassinate McNamara during his visit to South Vietnam. At first a visitor is likely to be both moved by this cult of Norman Morrison and made uncomfortable by it. Although the emotion of individuals is plainly unfeigned, it seems excessive, sentimental, and redolent of the hagiography of exemplary cardboard heroes that has been a regular feature of Stalinist and Maoist culture. But after the twentieth time that Norman Morrison's name was invoked (often shyly, always affectionately, with an evident desire to be friendly and gracious to *us*, who were Americans), I started understanding the very specific relation the Vietnamese have with Norman Morrison. The Vietnamese believe that the life of a people, its very will, is nourished and sustained by heroes. And Norman Morrison really is a hero, in a precise sense. (The Vietnamese don't, as I suspected at first, overestimate the actual impact of his sacrifice upon the conscience of America; far more than its practical efficacy, what matters to them is the moral success of his deed, its *completeness* as an act of self-transcendence.) Therefore, they're speaking quite accurately when they declare their "respect" for him and when they call him, as they often do, their "benefactor." Norman Morrison has become genuinely important for the Vietnamese, so much so that they can't comprehend that he mightn't be an equally important aliment of consciousness to us, three of their "American friends."

That very definition of us as friends, initially a source of some embarrassment and malaise, now seemed—another sign of the change in me—more comprehensible. Whereas at first I'd felt both moved, sometimes to tears, and constrained by the friendliness shown to us, eventually I could simply appreciate it, becoming more genuine and flexible in my own response. I surely had no grounds for suspecting the Vietnamese of duplicity, or for dismissing their attitude as naïve. Since, after all, I was a friend, why was it naïve or gullible of them to know that? Instead of being so amazed at their ability to transcend their situation as America's victims and our identity as citizens of the enemy nation, I began to imagine concretely how it was indeed possible for the Vietnamese, at this moment in their history, to welcome American citizens as friends. It was important, I realized, not to be abashed by all the small gifts and flowers thrust on us wherever we went. I'd minded that we weren't allowed to pay for anything during our stay—not even the numerous books I asked for or the cables I sent my son in New York every few days to let him know I was all right (despite my insistence that at least I be allowed to pay for these). Gradually, I could see it was just stingy of me to resist, or feel oppressed by, the material generosity of our hosts.

But the change didn't consist only in my becoming a more graceful recipient of Vietnamese generosity, a better audience for their elaborate courtesy. Here, too, there was something further to be understood; and through more contact with people in Vietnam, I discovered their politeness to be quite unlike "ours," and not only because there was so much more of it. In America and Europe, being polite (whether in large or small doses) always carries a latent hint of insincerity, a mild imputation of coercion. For us, politeness means conventions of amiable behavior people have agreed to practice, whether or not they "really" feel like it, because their "real" feelings aren't consistently civil or generous enough to guarantee a working social order. By definition, politeness is never truly honest; it testifies to the disparity between social behavior and authentic feeling. Perhaps this disparity, accepted in this part of the world as an article of faith concerning the human condition, is what gives us our taste for irony. Irony becomes essential as a mode of indicating the truth, a whole life-truth: namely, that we both mean and don't mean what we're saying or doing. I had originally been disconcerted by the absence of irony among the Vietnamese. But if I could renounce, at least imaginatively, my conviction of the inevitability of irony, the Vietnamese suddenly looked far less undecipherable. Their language didn't seem quite so imprisoning and simplistic, either. (For the development of ironic truths, one needs lots of words. Without irony, not so many words are required.)

The Vietnamese operate by another notion of civility than the one we're accustomed to, and that implies a shift in the meaning of honesty and sincerity. Honesty as it is understood in Vietnam bears little resemblance to the sense of honesty that has been elevated by secular Western culture virtually above all other values. In Vietnam, honesty and sincerity are functions of the dignity of the individual. A Vietnamese, by being sincere, reinforces and enhances his personal dignity. In this society, being sincere often means precisely forfeiting one's claim to dignity, to an attractive appearance; it means the willingness to be shameless. The difference is acute. This culture subscribes to an empirical or descriptive notion of sincerity, which measures whether a man is sincere by how fully and accurately his words mirror his hidden thoughts and feelings. The Vietnamese have a normative or prescriptive notion of sincerity. While our aim is to make the right alignment—correspondence—between one's words and behavior and one's inner life (on the assumption that the truth voiced by the speaker is ethically neutral, or rather is rendered ethically neutral or even praiseworthy by the speaker's willingness to avow it), theirs is to construct an appropriate relation between the speaker's words and behavior and his social identity. Sincerity, in Vietnam, means behaving in a manner *worthy* of one's role; sincerity is a mode of ethical aspiration.

Thus, it's off the point to speculate whether the warmth of Pham Van Dong during the hour conversation Bob, Andy, and I had with him in the late afternoon of May 16 was sincere in our sense, or whether the Prime Minister

"really" wanted to embrace us as we left his office, before
walking us out the front door and across the gravel
driveway to our waiting cars. He was sincere in the
Vietnamese sense: his behavior was attractive, it was becoming, it intended good. Nor is it quite right to ask
whether the Vietnamese "really" hate the Americans, even
though they say they don't; or to wonder why they don't
hate Americans, if indeed they do not. One basic unit of
Vietnamese culture is the extraordinary, beautiful gesture.
But gesture mustn't be interpreted in our sense—something put on, theatrical. The gestures a Vietnamese makes
aren't a performance external to his real personality. By
means of gestures, those acts brought off according to
whatever standards he affirms, his self is constituted. And
in certain cases, personality can be wholly redefined by a
single, unique gesture: for a person to do something finer
than he ever has done may promote him, without residue,
to a new level on which such acts are regularly possible.
(In Vietnam, moral ambition is a truth—an already
confirmed reality—in a way it isn't among us, because of
our psychological criteria of "the typical" and "the con-
sistent." This contrast sheds light on the quite different
role political and moral exhortation plays in a society like
Vietnam. Much of the discourse we would dismiss as
propagandistic or manipulative possesses a depth for the
Vietnamese to which we are insensitive.)

Vietnam—at least in its official view of itself—may
strike the secular Western eye as a society tremendously
overextended ethically, that is, psychologically. But such a
judgment depends entirely on our current, modest stand-

ards of how much virtue human beings are capable of. And Vietnam is, in many ways, an affront to these standards. I remember feeling just so affronted when, during the first afternoon of a two-day drive into mountainous Hoa Binh province north of Hanoi, we stopped briefly somewhere in the countryside to visit the grave of an American pilot. As we got out of our cars and walked off the road about fifty yards through the high grass, Oanh told us that it was the pilot of an F-105 brought down by a farmer with a rifle about a year ago. The pilot had failed to eject and crashed with his plane on this very spot; some villagers recovered his body from the wreckage. Coming into a clearing, we saw not a simple grave but an elevated mound decorated with chunks of the plane's engine and a crumpled piece of wing, like a Chamberlain sculpture, and with flowers, and topped by a wooden marker on which was written the pilot's name and the date of his death. I stood there some minutes feeling haunted, barely able to comprehend that initial act of burial, astonished by the look of the site and the evidence that it was still being looked after. And afterwards, when the vice-chairman of the province's administrative council, who was traveling in my car, explained that the pilot had been buried, and in "a coffin of good wood," so that his family in America could come after the war and take his body home, I felt almost undone. What is one to make of this amazing act? How could these people, who have had spouses and parents and children murdered by this pilot and his comrades (the load of one F-105, four canisters of CBU's, kills every unsheltered living creature within an area of one square kilometer), quietly take up their shovels and tastefully arrange his grave? What did they feel? Did they realize that whatever his objective guilt, he, just as much as their dead, was a precious, irreplaceable human being who should not have died? Could they pity him? Did they forgive him? But maybe these questions are misleading. What's likely is that the villagers thought burying the pilot was a beautiful (they would probably say "humane") thing to do—a standard that both overrides and transforms their personal feelings, so far as these might enter the matter.

Such transpersonal gestures are hard for a visitor to credit on their own terms. Certainly, I wasn't entirely able to put aside my own habitual understanding of how people function. Throughout the two weeks, I was continually tempted to frame psychological questions about the Vietnamese—all the while knowing how loaded such questions are with arbitrary, Western ethical assumptions. If it even makes sense to inquire, for instance, what "ego" is for the Vietnamese, I could observe that it doesn't take many of the expressive forms familiar to us. People in North Vietnam seem astonishingly calm, and though they talk of little else but the war, their discourse is singularly unmarked by hate. Even when they use the melodramatic Communist language of denunciation, it comes out sounding dutiful and a little flat. They talk of atrocities, the marrow of their history, with an almost gentle sorrow, and still with amazement. Can these things really have happened, their manner says. Did the French really disembowel that row of handcuffed plantation workers who had gone on strike, as the photograph we saw in the Revolutionary Museum shows? How can the Americans not be *ashamed* of what they're doing here? was the unspoken question that echoed throughout our tour of another, smaller "museum" in Hanoi devoted to a display of the various genocidal weapons used by the Americans on North Vietnam in the last three years. Indeed, I think, they don't quite understand—which, after all, is just the failure of understanding one might expect to find in a culture built on shame that's currently under attack by a culture whose energies come from deploying huge increments of guilt.

That Vietnam is a culture founded on shame probably accounts for much of what one sees (and does not see) there in the range of people's expressiveness. And my formation in a culture founded on guilt is surely one reason I found it hard to understand them. I would guess that guilt-cultures are typically prone to intellectual doubt and moral convolutedness, so that, from the point of view of guilt, all cultures founded on shame are indeed "naïve." The relation to moral demands tends to be much less ambivalently felt in shame-cultures, and collective action and the existence of public standards have an inherent validity they do not possess for us.

Prominent among these public standards in Vietnam is decorum—more generally, the concern for maintaining in all exchanges between people an exacting moral tone. I might have imagined this concern to be simply Asian if I hadn't already seen something of Cambodians and Laotians, in contrast with whom the Vietnamese are much more dignified and reserved, even prudish in their manner, and also more discreet in their dress. No matter how fiercely hot it gets, nowhere does one see in Vietnam (as one does throughout Cambodia and Laos) a man in shorts or without a shirt. Everyone is neatly, if shabbily, dressed from neck to ankles—women as well as men wear long trousers—and great value is placed on being clean. The pride of people in Na Phon when they showed us their two-stall brick and cement public latrine, the first such facility in the hamlet and completed just a day earlier, had to do with more than hygiene or convenience. The new latrine was a kind of moral victory. "All the water of the Eastern Sea could not wash away the dirt left by the enemy" is a saying that dates from one of the innumerable Vietnamese struggles against the Chinese, a war which began in 1418 and ended victoriously in 1427. No doubt the North Vietnamese regard with a similar anguish the three years of American assault: once again, and most horrendously, their country has been defiled. The moral metaphor of cleanliness and dirt is, of course, found almost universally, in all cultures; still, I felt it to be especially strong in Vietnam. Its strength is strikingly expressed in the eighteenth-century epic *Kieu,* the most famous work of Vietnamese literature. (The poem is studied in detail in the schools and recited often on the radio; practically every Vietnamese knows long passages from it by heart.) When the story begins, the heroine, Kieu, is a young girl. A young man sees her, falls in love with her, secretly and patiently courts her, but family duties suddenly call him away before he can explain. Believing herself abandoned and faced by a family crisis of her own, Kieu sells herself as a concubine to a rich man, to save her father from debtors' prison. Only after twenty years of mistreatment and degradation, in which she ends up in a brothel and from there escapes to become a bonze, is Kieu able to return home, where she meets again the man she loved. He asks her to marry him. In the long final scene, which takes place on their wedding night, Kieu tells her husband that, although she loves him deeply and has never enjoyed sexual relations with any other man, their marriage can't be consummated. He protests that her unfortunate life during their long separation means nothing to him; but she insists that she is not clean. Precisely as they love each other, she argues, they must make this sacrifice. Eventually, out of respect and love for her, he agrees. The poem ends with a description of the harmony and joy of their married life. To a Western sensibility, such a happy ending is hardly happy at all. We would rather have Kieu die of tuberculosis in the arms of her true love, just after they are reunited, than award them a lifetime together of renunciation. But to the Vietnamese, even today, the resolution of the story is both satisfying and just. What may appear to us as their being "closed," secretive, or unexpressive, I think, is partly that they are a remarkably fastidious people.

Needless to say, the standards of today are not the same as those proposed in *Kieu*. Sexual self-control, however, is still much admired. In present-day Vietnam, women and men work, eat, fight, and sleep together without raising any issue of sexual temptation. By now the Vietnamese understand that Westerners don't have the same standards of sexual propriety. Oanh, when he told me that it's very unusual for Vietnamese husbands and wives to be unfaithful to each other, even in circumstances of lengthy separation caused by war, said he knew marital fidelity was "not common" in the West. With an edge of self-mockery, he mentioned how shocked he was on one of his first trips to Europe—it was to Russia—to hear people at parties telling "indecent" jokes to each other. Now, he assured me, it bothers him less. With their incorrigible politeness, the Vietnamese have concluded that we arrange such matters differently. Thus, whenever Andy Kopkind, Bob Greenblatt, and I traveled in the countryside, no matter how primitive and small the sleeping accommodations, we were always given separate rooms (or something that passed for rooms); but on one of these trips, when we were accompanied by a nurse because Bob had become slightly ill in Hanoi the day before our departure, I noticed that the young, pretty nurse slept in the same room as our guides and drivers, who were all men. . . . Sexual self-discipline, I imagine, must be taken for granted in Vietnam. It's only a single aspect of the general demand made on the individual to maintain his dignity and to put himself at the disposal of others for the common good. In contrast to Laos and Cambodia, with their "Indian" or "southern" atmosphere that derives from an eclectic blend of Hindu and Buddhist influences, Vietnam presents the paradox of a country sharing the same severely tropical climate but living by the classical values—hard work, discipline, seriousness—of a country with a temperate or cold climate. This "northern" atmosphere is undoubtedly the legacy of those hordes of "Northern feudalists." (I also gathered that it is more attenuated in the southern region of the country. People in Hanoi describe the Saigonese as more easygoing, more emotional, more charming, but also less honest and sexually looser—in short, the conventional northern clichés about southerners.)

Thus, while the exacting demands the Vietnamese make upon themselves, in their present form, are undoubtedly reinforced by the paramilitary ethos of a left-revolutionary society under invasion, their basic form has deep historical roots, particularly in the Confucian as distinct from the Buddhist strands in Vietnamese culture. In some societies, notably China, these two traditions have been experienced as sharply antagonistic. But in Vietnam, I suspect, they have not. Most Vietnamese, of course, apart from a large Catholic minority, are Buddhists. Even though we saw mostly old people praying in the pagodas, a good deal of domestic ritual still takes place (we saw altars in many homes); beyond that, there appears to be a considerable secular continuity with Buddhist values. Nevertheless, whatever in Vietnam persists of the Buddhist ethos—with its fatalism, its intellectual playfulness, its stress on charity —seems quite compatible with the ethos of discipline characteristic of Confucianism. The behavior of the Vietnamese reflects the Confucian idea that both the body politic and an individual's well-being depend on cultivating the rules of appropriate and just behavior. Also intact is the Confucian view expressed by Hsün Tzu: "All rules of decorum and righteousness are the product of the acquired virtue of the sage and not the products of the nature of man." This Confucian idea of a people's dependence on its sages partly explains the veneration felt by the Vietnamese for Ho Chi Minh, their sage-poet-leader. But only partly. As indeed the Vietnamese often insist, their regard for Ho has nothing in common with the mindless adulation surrounding Mao today. Ho's birthday is mainly an annual occasion for the North Vietnamese to show their good taste, the delicacy of their feeling toward him. "We love and respect our leader," commented the monthly journal *Hoc Tap* on Ho's birthday last year, "but we do not deify him." Far from treating him like the usual bigger-than-life, heroic, all-wise leader, people I met spoke of Ho as if they knew him personally, and what fascinates and stirs them is their sense of him as a real man. Humorous anecdotes illustrating his modesty and shyness are legion. People find him charming, even a little eccentric. And they are moved when they speak of him, reminiscing about his years of privation in exile and his sufferings in Chinese jails throughout the 1930's, and worrying over his physical frailty. *Bac Ho,* Uncle Ho, is no special title, with Orwellian Big Brother overtones, but ordinary courtesy; a Vietnamese of any age addresses someone of an older generation to whom he's not related as "Uncle" or "Aunt." (Swedish has the same usage, except that *tant* and *farbror* are used only by children or young people to address adults who are strangers, and wouldn't be said by a middle-aged person to a seventy-year-old.) The feeling for Ho Chi Minh, an intimate affection and gratitude, is only the apex of the feeling that exists between people in a small, beleaguered nation who are able to regard each other as members of one big family. Indeed, almost all the virtues admired by the Vietnamese —such as frugality, loyalty, self-sacrifice, and sexual fidelity—have, as their basic supporting metaphor, the authority of family life. Here is still another feature pointing back to Confucianism—as distinct from Buddhism, which attaches the highest prestige to monastic separation from society and the renunciation of family ties—and away from the austerity and "puritanism" of Vietnamese culture considered as something relatively new, the graft of revolutionary ideology. (Considered as "Marxist-Leninist *thought*," Vietnamese Communism seems conveniently vague and outstandingly platitudinous.) Though a visitor is tempted to attribute the extraordinary discipline of the country in large measure to the influence of Communist ideology, it's probably the other way around: that the influence of Communist moral demands derives its authority from the indigenous Vietnamese respect for a highly moralized social and personal order.

But I am making the Vietnamese sound more solemn than they are, when actually what is particularly noticeable is the grace with which these ends are pursued. In conversation, the Vietnamese are low-keyed; even in public meetings, they are laconic and not particularly hortatory. It is hard to recognize the passionate consciousness when it lacks the signs of passion as we know them—such as agitation and pathos. One realizes that these are people living through the most exalted moment of their consciousness, the climax of more than a quarter of a century of continuous struggle. They have already beaten the French against incredible odds. (The French first brought napalm to Vietnam. Between 1950 and 1954, eighty percent of the French budget for the war was paid for by the United States.) Now, even more incredibly, they've demonstrated they can endure whatever punishment the Americans can inflict on them, and still cohere and prosper as a people, while in the South the National Liberation Front is steadily extending its support and control of territory. Yet most of the time this mood of exaltation has to be inferred by the sympathetic observer—not because the Vietnamese are unemotional, but because of their habitual emotional tact, a cultural principle of the conservation of emotional energy. We were told that in heavily bombed places in the countryside it's common for the farmers to take their coffins with them each day when they go to the rice fields, so that if someone dies, he can be buried right then while the others continue working. In the evacuated schools, children pack up their personal belongings and bedding before they leave the dormitory hut each morning for classes and pile the tiny bundles neatly in the nearest dirt shelter, in case there is a bombing raid during the day and the hut burns down; each evening they take their bundles out of the shelter, unpack them, and set up the dormitory again. . . . More than once, observing the incredible matter-of-factness of the Vietnamese, I thought of the Jews' more wasteful and more brilliant style of meeting their historical destiny of chronic suffering and struggle. One advantage of the Vietnamese over the Jews as a martyr people, perhaps, is simply that of any culture dominated by the peasant type over a culture that has crystallized into an urban bourgeoisie. Unlike the Jews, the Vietnamese belong to a culture whose various psychic types have not yet reached a high degree of articulation (forcing them to reflect upon *each other*). It is also the advantage of having a history, albeit mainly of cruel persecution, that is anchored to a land with which people identify themselves, rather than simply (and, therefore, complicatedly) to an "identity."

The Jews' manner of experiencing their suffering was direct, emotional, persuasive. It ran the gamut from stark declamation to ironic self-mockery. It attempted to engage the sympathy of others. At the same time, it projected a despair over the difficulties of engaging others. The source of the Jewish stubbornness, of their miraculous talent for survival, is their surrender to a complex kind of pessimism. Perhaps something like the Jewish (and also "Western") style of overt expressive suffering was what I unconsciously expected to find when I came to Vietnam. That would explain why at first I took for opaqueness and naïveté the quite different way the Vietnamese have of experiencing a comparably tragic history.

It took me a while, for instance, to realize that the Vietnamese were genuinely constrained by a kind of modesty about showing us the unspeakable sufferings they have endured. Even when describing the American atrocities, they hastened to emphasize—almost as if it would be bad taste not to—that the full horror of America's war on Vietnam couldn't be seen anywhere in the North. For that, they said, one must see "what is happening to our brothers in the South." We heard the statistics of civilian casualties since Feb. 7, 1965: sixty percent of all people killed are women and children; twenty percent of those killed and seriously wounded are elderly people. We were taken to see towns where formerly no fewer than twenty thousand and as many as eighty thousand people lived, in which not a single building was standing. We saw photographs of bodies riddled with pellets from fragmentation bombs or charred by incendiary weapons (besides napalm, the Americans also drop white phosphorus, Thermit, and magnesium on the Vietnamese). We met briefly with some forlorn victims of "the escalation," among them a girl of twenty-four whose husband and mother-in-law and children had been killed in a single raid, and an elderly Mother Superior and two young nuns who were the only survivors of the bombing of a Catholic convent located just south of Hanoi. Nevertheless, our North Vietnamese hosts seemed anything but eager to ply us with atrocities. They seemed more pleased to tell us, as we visited ruin after ruin, when there had been no casualties—as was the case when the new 170-bed hospital outside of Hoa Binh City was destroyed. (The hospital had been evacuated just before the first raid in September 1967; it was bombed several times afterwards and of course has never been reoccupied.) The impression the Vietnamese prefer to give, and do, is of a peaceful, viable, optimistic society. Ho Chi Minh has even given, in a speech after August 1945, a five-point recipe "for making life optimistic": each person must (1) be good in politics, (2) be able to draw or paint, (3) know music, (4) practice some sport, and

(5) know at least one foreign language. Thus, by optimism among the Vietnamese, I mean not only their implacable conviction that they are going to win, but their
espousal of optimism as a form of understanding, the
emphasis placed throughout the whole society on continuous improvement.

Indeed, one of the most striking aspects of Vietnam is
the positiveness of their approach to almost any problem.
As Professor Buu, the Minister of Higher Education,
remarked without a trace of irony: "The Americans have
taught us a lot. For instance, we see that what's necessary
for education is not beautiful buildings, like the brand-
new Polytechnic School in Hanoi which we had to aban-
don in 1965 with the start of the escalation. When we
went into the jungle and built the decentralized schools,
education improved. We'd like better food and more col-
orful clothes, of course, but in these three years we've
learned one can do many things without them. We don't
regard them as fundamental, though very important all
the same." Among the advantages, he said, in having been
forced to evacuate the colleges of Hanoi into the countryside were that the college students had to put up their new
school buildings themselves and learn how to grow their
own food (every evacuated school or factory forms a new
community and is asked not to be parasitic on the nearest
village but to become self-sufficient on the level of a
subsistence economy). Through these ordeals, "a new
man" is being formed. Somehow, incredibly, the Vietnamese appreciate the assets of their situation, particularly
its effect on character. When Ho Chi Minh said that

bombing heightens the "spirit" of people, he meant more
than a stiffening of morale. There is the belief that the
war has effected a permanent improvement in the moral
level of people. For instance, for a family to be uprooted
and have all its possessions destroyed (many families have
relics going back ten centuries) has always been considered in Vietnam the worst possible fate, but now that
just this has happened to so many tens of thousands of
families, people have discovered the positive advantages
of being stripped of everything: that one becomes more
generous, less attached to "things." (This is the theme of
a movie I saw, *The Forest of Miss Tham*, in which at the
end, to facilitate the repair of a truck route after a bombing, an old peasant volunteers to cut down the two trees
he has spent his whole life growing.) The bombing has also
been, for instance, an occasion for developing people's
poise and articulateness and administrative talents. Each
village or hamlet, through an elected team, does its own
reporting on the bombing; in Hanoi and Haiphong, several residents from each street are delegated to make out
detailed reports. I remember, on our inspection of the
bombed areas of Hanoi, receiving such a report from the
leader of the "investigation team" of Quan Than Street
(two kilometers from our hotel), an elderly uneducated
worker who, since he was elected to this job by his neighbors, had learned a whole new set of skills. The war has
made people cleverer and also democratized the use of intel-
ligence, since everybody has essentially the same task: pro-
tecting the country, repelling the aggressors. Throughout
North Vietnam, self-help plus cooperation has become the

regular form of social and economic life. This may sound like the conventional code of a socialist economy applied in an underdeveloped country. But North Vietnam is not just one more small, economically backward member of the Third World, afflicted with the standard handicaps of an overspecialized economy (imposed by colonial rule), illiteracy, disease, and hard-to-assimilate tribal peoples culturally anterior to the majority population. (Vietnam has sixty "ethnic minorities.") It is a country that has literally been gashed and poisoned and leveled by steel, toxic chemicals, and fire. Under these circumstances, self-sufficiency would hardly be enough—were it not for the remarkable ability of the Vietnamese somehow to nourish themselves on disaster.

People there put it much more simply: it's just a question of being sufficiently ingenious. The overwhelming superiority of the United States in manpower, weapons, and resources and the extent of the devastation already wrought on their country pose a definite "problem," as the Vietnamese often said, but one they fully expect to solve by their unlimited and "creative" devotion to work. Everywhere we went, we saw evidence of the tremendous output of toil needed to keep North Vietnam going. Work is, as it were, evenly distributed over the whole surface of the country—like the huge wooden crates lying, unguarded, on the edges of sidewalks on many streets in Hanoi ("our evacuated warehouses," Oanh said) and on country roads, or the piles of tools and other material left in the open alongside the railroad tracks so that repair of the track can start within minutes after a bombing. Never-

theless, willing as the Vietnamese are to rebuild the country inch by inch with shovel and hammer, they have a
rather elegant sense of priorities. For instance, it was usual
for the craters blasted in rice fields by the B-52's to be
filled in by the farmers within days after the raid. But we
saw several craters, made by 2,000- and 3,000-pound
bombs, so big it had been judged that the time and labor
needed to fill them would be prohibitive; these had been
converted into fish-breeding ponds. Though the on-going
and endless work of repairing bomb-damaged sites and
facilities or constructing new, better-protected ones con-
sumes most of their energies now, the Vietnamese think a
great deal about the future. Mindful of their postwar need
for people with sophisticated skills, the Vietnamese have
not mobilized teachers and professors or any of the
200,000 students in colleges and vocational schools; indeed, the number of students enrolled in programs of
higher education has steadily risen since 1965. Architects
have already drawn up plans for the completely new cities
(including Hanoi, which the North Vietnamese fully expect to be razed before the Americans finally withdraw)
that must be built after the war.

A visitor may conclude that this work, for all its ingenuity, is mainly conservative in purpose—the means
whereby the society can survive—and only secondarily
expresses a revolutionary vision—the instrument of a society bent on radical change. But the two purposes, I think,
cannot be separated. The war seems to have democratized
North Vietnam more profoundly, and radically, than any
of the socialist economic reforms undertaken between

1954 and 1965. For instance, the war has broken down one of the few strong articulations in Vietnamese society: between the city and the country. (Peasants still make up eighty percent of the North Vietnamese population.) When the American bombing started, over a million and a half people left Hanoi, Haiphong, and other smaller cities and scattered throughout the countryside, where they have been living now for several years; the population of Hanoi alone dropped from around one million before 1965 to less than 200,000. And this migration, several Vietnamese told me, has already effected a marked change in manners and sensibility, both among peasants who have had to absorb a colony of motley refugees with urban habits and tastes, and among people from Hanoi or Haiphong, many of whom knew nothing about the starkly primitive conditions of daily existence that still prevail in the villages and hamlets but find themselves thriving psychically on physical austerity and the community-mindedness of rural life.

The war has also democratized the society by destroying most of the modest physical means as well as restricting the social space Vietnam had at its disposal for differentiated kinds of production (I include everything from industry to the arts). Thus, more and more people are working at all kinds of activities at the same level—with their bare hands. Each small, low building in the complexes of evacuated schools that have been set up throughout the countryside had to be made in the simplest way: mud walls and a straw roof. All those kilometers of neat trenches connecting and leading away from every building, to get the children out in case of attack, had to be painstakingly dug out of the red clay. The omnipresent bomb shelters—throughout Hanoi, in each village and hamlet, at intervals on the side of every road, in every tilled field—had to be put up, one by one, by people living nearby, in their spare time. (Since 1965, the Vietnamese have dug more than 50,000 kilometers of trenches and constructed, for a population of 17,000,000, more than 21,000,000 bomb shelters.) Late one night, on our way back to Hanoi from a trip to the north, we visited a decentralized factory housed in crude sheds at the foot of a mountain. While several hundred women and young boys were operating the machines by the light of kerosene lamps, a dozen men using only hammers were widening the walls of a small adjacent cave to make a shelter safe from bombing for the biggest machinery. Almost everything in North Vietnam has to be done manually, with a minimum of tools. Time enough to wonder what the vaunted aid from Russia and China amounts to: however much there is of it, it's scarcely enough. The country is pitifully lacking in such elementary hospital equipment as sterilizers and X-ray machines, in typewriters, in basic tools like lathes and pneumatic drills and welding machines; there seem to be plenty of bicycles and quite a few transistor radios, but books of all kinds, paper, pens, phonographs, clocks, and cameras are very scarce; the most modest consumer goods are virtually nonexistent. Clothing, too, exists only in a limited supply. A Vietnamese is lucky if he owns two sets of clothes and one pair of shoes; rationing allows each person six meters of cotton fabric a year. (The cotton comes in only a few colors and most garments are almost identically cut: black trousers and white blouses for the women; tan, gray, or beige trousers and tan or white shirts for the men. Ties are never worn, and jackets only rarely.) Even the clothes of very high officials are frayed, dully stained, shiny from repeated washings. Dr. Thach, cousin of the former puppet emperor Bao Dai and, before throwing in his lot with the revolution, one of the richest landowners in Vietnam, mentioned that he hasn't had any new clothes in two years. Food is very short, too, though no one starves. Industrial workers get a monthly ration of 24 kilos of rice; everyone else, including the highest government officials, gets 13.5 kilos a month.

Lacking almost everything, the Vietnamese are forced to put everything they do have to use, sometimes multiple use. Part of this ingenuity is traditional; for example, the Vietnamese make an astonishing number of things out of bamboo—houses, bridges, irrigation devices, scaffolding, carrying poles, cups, tobacco pipes, furniture. But there are many new inventions. Thus, American planes have become virtual mines in the sky. (The supply is still far from cut off. During our stay in Hanoi, the Vietnamese bagged a dozen of the unmanned reconnaissance planes that have been flying over several times a day since March 31; and they get more planes below the 19th parallel, where the air attack is more intense now than at any time before the "limited bombing pause.") Each plane that's shot down is methodically taken apart. The tires are cut up to make the rubber sandals that most people wear. Any component of the engine that's still intact is modified to be reused as part of a truck motor. The body of the plane is dismantled, and the metal is melted down to be made into tools, small machine parts, surgical instruments, wire, spokes for bicycle wheels, combs, ashtrays, and of course the famous numbered rings given as presents to visitors. Every last nut, bolt, and screw from the plane is used. The same holds for anything else the Americans drop. In several hamlets we visited, the bell hanging from a tree which summoned people to meetings or sounded the air-raid alert was the casing of an unexploded bomb. Being shown through the infirmary of a Thai hamlet, we saw that the protective canopy of the operating room, relocated, since the bombing, in a rock grotto, was a flare parachute.

In these circumstances, the notion of a "people's war" is no mere propagandistic slogan but takes on a real concreteness, as does that favorite hope of modern social planners, decentralization. A people's war means the total, voluntary, generous mobilization of every able-bodied person in the country, so that everyone is available for any task. It also means the division of the country into an indefinite number of small, self-sufficient communities which can survive isolation, make decisions, and continue contributing to production. People on a *local* level are expected, for instance, to solve any kind of problem put to them as the aftermath of enemy bombing.

To observe in some of its day-to-day functioning a society based on the principle of total use is particularly impressive to someone who comes from a society based on maximal waste. An unholy dialectic is at work here, in which the big wasteful society dumps its garbage, its partly unemployable proletarian conscripts, its poisons, and its bombs upon a small, virtually defenseless, frugal society whose citizens, those fortunate enough to survive, then go about picking up the debris, out of which they fashion materials for daily use and self-defense.

The principle of total use applies not only to things but to thoughts as well, and grasping this helped me to stop mechanically chafing at the intellectual flatness of Vietnamese discourse. As each material object must be made to go a long way, so must each idea. Vietnamese leaders specialize in an economical, laconic wisdom. Take the saying of Ho, repeated to us often: "Nothing is more precious than independence and liberty." Not until I'd heard the quote many many times did I actually consider it. But when I did, I thought, yes, it really does say a great deal. One could indeed, as the Vietnamese have, live spiritually from that simple sentence for a long time. The Vietnamese regard Ho not as a thinker but as a man of action; his words are for use. The same standard applies to the iconography of the Vietnamese struggle, which is hardly outstanding for either visual or ideological subtlety. (Of course, the utilitarian principle doesn't work equally well in all contexts, as evidenced by the rather low level of Vietnamese visual art, with the exception of posters. In contrast to the poor development not only of painting but of film, prose fiction, and dance as well, poetry and theatre seemed to me the only arts in a sophisticated condition, as arts, in Vietnam now.) The principle of getting maximal use from everything may partly explain why there are still quite a few pictures of Stalin in North Vietnam, hanging on the wall in some but hardly all government offices, factories, and schools. Stalin is the traditional figure on the right in the tintype pantheon Marx-Engels-Lenin-Stalin, and the Vietnamese lack both time and incentive for symbolic controversy. The composition of that quartet represents a form of politeness to the leading country and titular head of the "socialist camp" which was installed when the present government came to power in 1954. People in North Vietnam are perfectly well aware that the picture is out of date in 1968, and many North Vietnamese appeared to me to have grave reservations about the Soviet Union's domestic and foreign policies, even the character of its people. (Ho Chi Minh, whose picture is rarely to be seen in public buildings, pointedly refused the Lenin Prize a few years ago.) But whatever the Vietnamese, especially in Hanoi, might think, or even express privately, about the Russians—that they are collaborating with the Americans, that they don't genuinely back Vietnam's struggle, that they've abandoned the ideals of genuine Communism and of world revolution, that they're prone to be drunks and boors—does not yet invalidate the old icon. It remains, at least for the present, as a polite tribute to the *idea* of unity and solidarity among the Communist countries.

It's all part of the Vietnamese style, which seems guided by an almost principled avoidance of "heaviness," of making more complications than are necessary. No one can fail to credit the Vietnamese with subtlety in planning large-scale actions, as evidenced in the fabulous strategic sense of General Giap. But directness and plainness remain the rule when it comes to expressing something or making a gesture, and not out of any deeper artfulness. It was my impression that the Vietnamese, as a culture, genuinely believe that life is simple. They also believe, incredible as it may seem considering their present situation, that life is full of joy. Joy is to be discerned behind what is already so remarkable: the ease and total lack of self-pity with which people worked a backbreaking number of hours, or daily faced the possibility of their own death and the death of those they love. The phenomena of existential agony, of alienation, just don't appear among the Vietnamese—probably in part because they lack our kind of "ego," and our endowment of free-floating guilt. Of course, it's hard for a visitor to take all this at face value. I spent much of my early time in Vietnam wondering what lay "behind" the Vietnamese's apparent psychic equilibrium. The kind of seriousness—identified, Confucian-style, with unselfishness—that is deeply ingrained in Vietnamese culture is something which visitors from the Western capitalist world, equipped with their tools of psychological debunking, can hardly recognize, much less fully credit. Right away, the delicate build of the Vietnamese and their sheer physical gracefulness can set a gawky, big-boned American on edge. The Vietnamese behave with an unfaltering personal dignity that we tend to find suspect, either naïve or sham. And they appear so singularly and straightforwardly involved with the virtue of courage, and with the ideal of a noble, brave life. We live in an age marked by the discrediting of the heroic effort; hence, the awareness most people in this society have of their lives, whether they are appalled by it or not, as stale and flat. But in Vietnam one is confronted by a whole people possessed by a belief in what Lawrence called "the subtle, lifelong validity of the heroic impulse." Educated urban Americans, imbued with a sense of the decline of the heroic spirit, must find it especially difficult to perceive what animates the Vietnamese, to correlate the "known" historical dossier of their long patient struggle to liberate their country with what can really be "believed" about people.

Ultimately, the difficulty encountered visiting North Vietnam reflects the crisis of credulity that is endemic in Western post-industrial society. Not only do the Vietnamese have virtues that thoughtful people in this part of the world simply don't believe in any more. They also mix virtues that we consider incompatible. For instance, we think war to be by its very nature "dehumanizing." But North Vietnam is simultaneously a martial society, completely mobilized for armed struggle, and a deeply civil society which places great value on gentleness and the demands of the heart. One of the more astonishing instances of Vietnamese concern for the heart, related to me by Phan, is the treatment accorded the thousands of prostitutes rounded up after the liberation of Hanoi from the French in 1954. They were put in charge of the Women's Union, which set up rehabilitation centers for them in the countryside, where they first passed months being elaborately pampered. Fairy tales were read to them; they were taught children's games and sent out to play. "That,"

Phan explained, "was to restore their innocence and give them faith again in man. You see, they had seen such a terrible side of human nature. The only way for them to forget that was to become little children again." Only after this period of mothering were they taught to read and write, instructed in a trade by which they could support themselves, and given dowries to improve their chances of eventually marrying. There seems no doubt that people who can think up such therapy really have a different moral imagination than we have. And as the quality of Vietnamese love differs from ours, so does the nature of their hate. Of course, the Vietnamese hate the Americans in some sense—but not as Americans would, if we had been subjected to equivalent punishment at the hands of a superior power. The North Vietnamese genuinely care about the welfare of the hundreds of captured American pilots and give them bigger rations than the Vietnamese population gets, "because they're bigger than we are," as a Vietnamese army officer told me, "and they're used to more meat than we are." People in North Vietnam really do believe in the goodness of man ("People in every country are good," Ho said in 1945, "only the governments are bad"), and in the perennial possibility of rehabilitating the morally fallen, among whom they include implacable enemies, even the Americans. In spite of all the stiff words disseminated by the Vietnamese, it's impossible not to be convinced by the genuineness of these concerns.

Still, apart from the general problem of credulity a Western visitor brings to a society like Vietnam, one may be

doubly wary of any deeply positive reaction to the Vietnamese. The moment one begins to be affected by the
moral beauty of the Vietnamese, not to mention their
physical grace, a derisive inner voice starts calling it phony
sentimentality. Understandably, one fears succumbing to
that cut-rate sympathy for places like Vietnam which,
lacking any real historical or psychological understanding,
becomes another instance of the ideology of primitivism.
The revolutionary politics of many people in capitalist
countries is only a new guise for the old conservative
culture-criticism: posing against overcomplex, hypocriti-
cal, devitalized, urban society choking on affluence the
idea of a simple people living the simple life in a decentralized, uncoercive, passionate society with modest
material means. As eighteenth-century *philosophes* pic-
tured such a pastoral ideal in the Pacific islands or among
the American Indians, and German romantic poets supposed it to have existed in ancient Greece, late twentieth-
century intellectuals in New York and Paris are likely to
locate it in the exotic revolutionary societies of the Third
World. If some of what I've written evokes the very cliché
of the Western left-wing intellectual idealizing an agrar-
ian revolution that I was so set on not being, I must reply
that a cliché is a cliché, truth is truth, and direct experience
is—well—something one repudiates at one's peril. In the
end I can only avow that, armed with these very self-
suspicions, I found, through direct experience, North Vietnam to be a place which, in many respects, *deserves* to be
idealized.

But, having stated my admiration for the Vietnamese

(people, society) as bluntly and vulnerably as I can, I should emphasize that none of this amounts to a claim that North Vietnam is a model of a just state. One has only to recall the more notorious crimes committed by the present government: for example, the persecution of the Trotskyist faction and the execution of its leaders in 1946; and the forcible collectivization of agriculture in 1956, the brutalities and injustices of which high officials have recently admitted. Still, a foreigner should try to avoid padding out the lamentable facts with a reflex reaction to words. Upon learning that in North Vietnam today everyone belongs to at least one "organization" (usually several), a non-Communist visitor is likely to assume that the Vietnamese must be regimented and deprived of personal liberty. With the rise to dominance of the ideology of the bourgeoisie in the last two centuries, people in Europe and America have learned to associate membership in public organizations with becoming "depersonalized," and to identify achievement of the most valuable human goals with the autonomy of private life. But this apparently isn't how the threat of depersonalization arises in Vietnam; there, people rather experience themselves as dehumanized or depersonalized when they are not bound to each other in regular forms of collectivity. Again, a visitor of the independent Left will probably wince each time the Vietnamese mention "the Party." (The 1946 constitution does allow for a plurality of political groupings, and there is a Socialist Party and a Democratic Party, both of which publish weekly newspapers and have some representation in the government. But *Lao Dong,* the Workers Party, with nearly a hundred members on its Central Committee, is "the Party"; it runs the country, and the candidates it proposes are overwhelmingly favored by the electoral system.) But the preference for government by a single party of newly independent countries which have never known multi-party democracy is a fact that merits a more discriminating response than automatic disapproval. Several Vietnamese I met themselves brought up the dangers of single-party rule and claimed that in spite of these dangers the Workers Party had proved it deserves to hold power by being responsive to the concrete local demands of people. For the Vietnamese, "the Party" simply means the effective leadership of the country—from Ho Chi Minh, founder of the independent nation and of the Party (in 1930), to the young cadre just out of the Party School who comes to a village under bombardment to show its inhabitants how to build shelters or volunteers to live in the high mountains, among the Meo or Muong minorities, and teach them how to read and write. Of course, this conception of the Party as a vast corps of skilled, ethically impeccable, mostly unpaid public servants, tutoring and working alongside people in all their activities, sharing their hardships, doesn't exempt the Vietnamese system from terrible abuses. But neither does it preclude the possibility that the present system functions humanely, with genuine substantive democracy, much of the time.

In any case, I noticed that the word "democracy" was frequently invoked in Vietnam, far more often than in any other Communist country I've visited, including Cuba. The Vietnamese claim that democracy has deep roots in their culture, specifically in the customs of a fiercely independent peasantry. ("The law of the king must be subordinate to the law of the village," runs an old proverb.) Even in the past, Dr. Thach said, the form of the regime—kings and mandarins—was authoritarian, but its content—the traditions of village life—was democratic. Whether or not this account stands up to objective scrutiny, it's interesting that the Vietnamese *think* it true that their country is, and always has been, democratic. North Vietnam is the only Communist country I know in which people regularly praise the United States for being, after all and despite everything, "a great democracy." (As I've suggested, the Vietnamese don't show a very advanced command of Marxist thinking and critical analysis.) All this, myth as well as reality, must be taken into consideration when evaluating the nature of public institutions in North Vietnam and their role in promoting or discouraging individuality. The life of an institution cannot be appraised by examining a blueprint of its structure; run under the auspices of different feelings, similar structures can have a quite different quality. For instance, when love enters into the substance of social relations, the connection of people to a single party need not be dehumanizing. Though it's second nature for me to suspect the government of a Communist country of being oppressive and rigid, if not worse, most of my preconceptions about the misuses of state power in North Vietnam were really an abstraction. Against the abstract suspiciousness I must set (and be overruled by) what I actually saw when I was there—that the North Vietnamese genuinely love and admire their leaders; and, even more inconceivable to us, that the government loves the people. I remember the poignant, intimate tones in Pham Van Dong's voice as he described the sufferings the Vietnamese have endured in the last quarter of a century and their heroism, decency, and essential innocence. Seeing for the first time in my life a prime minister praising the moral character of his country's people with tears in his eyes has modified my ideas about the conceivable relations between rulers and ruled, and given me a more complex reaction to what I would ordinarily dismiss as mere propaganda.

For while no dearth of propaganda is put out by the North Vietnamese, what makes one despair is that this propaganda conveys so poorly, insensitively, and unconvincingly the most admirable qualities of the society built since 1954. Anyone who consults the publications about North Vietnam (on education, public health, the new role of women, literature, war crimes, etc.) issued in English and French by the Foreign Languages Press in Hanoi will not only get virtually nothing of the delicate texture of North Vietnamese society but be positively misled by the bombastic, shrill, and overly general character of these texts. Toward the close of my stay I mentioned to several government people that foreigners, reading these books and press releases, couldn't possibly form an idea of what North Vietnam is like, and explained my general impression that their revolution is being betrayed by its language. Though the Vietnamese I talked to seemed aware of the problem—they indicated I wasn't the first foreign visitor to tell them this—I felt they're far from knowing how to solve it. (I learned that Pham Van Dong had made a speech three years ago criticizing "the disease of rhetoric" that he charged was rife among the political cadres and appealing for an "improvement" of the Vietnamese language. But the only concrete advice he gave was that people spend less time talking about politics and more time reading classical Vietnamese literature.)

Can North Vietnam really be such an exceptional place? That's a question I have no way of answering. But I do know that North Vietnam, while definitely no Shangri-La, is a truly remarkable country; that the North Vietnamese is an extraordinary human being, and in ways not accounted for by the well-known fact that any keen struggle, a really desperate crisis, usually brings out the best (if not the worst) in people and promotes a euphoria of comradeship. What is admirable in the Vietnamese goes deeper than that. The Vietnamese are "whole" human beings, not "split" as we are. Inevitably, such people are likely to give outsiders the impression of great "simplicity." But while the Vietnamese are stripped down, they are hardly simple in any sense that grants us the right to patronize them.

It is *not* simple to be able to love calmly, to trust without ambivalence, to hope without self-mockery, to act courageously, to perform arduous tasks with unlimited resources of energy. In this society, a few people are able just faintly to imagine all these as achievable goals— though only in their private life. But in Vietnam the very distinction taken for granted here between the public and the private has not been strongly developed. This indis-

tinct separation between public and private among the
Vietnamese also informs their pragmatic, verbally and
conceptually meager style of making their revolution. By
way of contrast, the acute sense of the discontinuity of
private and public in the West may partly explain the
amount of talk, often very interesting talk, that accom-
panies every revolutionary gesture.* In our society, talk is
perhaps the most intricately developed expression of
private individuality. Conducted at this high pitch of
development, talking becomes a double-edged activity:
both an aggressive act and an attempted embrace. Thus
talk often testifies to the poverty or inhibition of our
feelings; it flourishes as a substitute for more organic
connections between people. (When people really love, or
are genuinely in touch with themselves, they tend to shut
up.) But Vietnam is a culture in which people have not

---

* What brings about genuine revolutionary change is the shared experience of revolutionary *feelings*—not rhetoric, not the discovery of social
injustice, not even intelligent analysis, and not any action considered in
itself. And one can indeed "talk" revolutions away, by a disproportion between consciousness and verbalization, on the one hand, and the amount
of practical *will,* on the other. (Hence the failure of the recent revolution
in France. The French students talked—and very beautifully, too—instead
of reorganizing the administration of the captured universities. Their
staging of street demonstrations and confrontations with the police was
conceived as a rhetorical or symbolic, rather than a practical, act; it too
was a kind of talking.)

In our society, "idealistic" tends to mean "disorganized"; "militant"
tends to mean merely "emotional." Most of the people in Europe and the
Americas who are quite vociferous in their denunciations of the society in
which they live are profoundly confused and thoughtless not only about
what they would prefer instead but about any plan for actually taking
power so radical change might be effected. Indeed, revolution in the
Western capitalist countries seems, more often than not, to be an activity
expressly designed never to succeed. For many people, it is an *a*social
activity, a form of action designed for the assertion of individuality against
the body politic. It is the ritual activity of outsiders, rather than of people
united by a passionate bond to their country.

got the final devastating point about talking, have not gauged the subtle, ambivalent resources of language—because they don't experience as we do the isolation of a "private self." Talk is still a rather plain instrumentality for them, a less important means of being connected with their environment than direct feeling, love.

The absence of the sharp distinction between public and private spheres also allows the Vietnamese a relation to their country that must seem exotic to us. It is open to the Vietnamese to love their country passionately, every inch of it. One can't exaggerate the fervor of their patriotic passion and their intense attachment to particular places. Most people, I noticed, volunteer quickly where they are from, with a special melancholy if they were born in the South and have therefore been prevented from returning there for many years. And I remember Oanh describing his childhood on his uncle's fishing boat in Ha Long Bay, a famous resort area during the French colonial period. (Oanh recalled the excitement he felt as a small boy in the late 1920's when Paulette Goddard spent a holiday there.) But when Oanh had gone on for a while about the splendors of the rock formations in the bay, now heavily bombed, he stopped, almost apologetically, to say something like: Of course your Rocky Mountains must be very beautiful, too.

But is it possible to feel like that about America now? That was something I often debated with the Vietnamese. They assured me that I must love America just as much as they love Vietnam. It's my patriotism that makes me oppose my country's foreign policy; I want to preserve the honor of the country I cherish above all others. There was some truth in what they said: all Americans—alas—believe that America is special, or ought to be. But I knew I didn't feel the positive emotion that Vietnamese attributed to me. Outrage and disappointment, yes. Love, no. Putting it in the baby language they and I shared (which I'd become rather skillful at), I explained: it's hard to love America right now, because of the violence which America is exporting all over the world; and given that the interests of humanity come before those of any particular people, a decent American today must be an internationalist first and a patriot second. Once at the Writers Union, when I had made this point (and not for the first time, so my voice may have been a little plaintive), a young poet answered me soothingly in English: "We are patriots, but in a happy way. You have more suffering in your patriotism." Sometimes they seemed to understand, but more often they didn't. Perhaps the difficulty is that, as I've already mentioned, they're quite fond of America themselves. People in Vietnam appear to take for granted that the United States *is* in many ways the greatest country in the world: the richest, the most advanced technologically, the most alive culturally, the most powerful, even the most free. They are not only endlessly curious about America—Oanh said several times how much he longs to visit the States as soon as the war is over—but genuinely admiring. I have described earlier the avidity of the poets and novelists for American literature. Pham Van Dong mentioned respectfully "your Declaration of Independence," from which Ho Chi Minh quoted when he declared the independence of Vietnam from the French on September 2, 1945. Hoang Tung, the editor of the principal daily paper, *Nhan Dan,* spoke of his "love" for the United States and praised to us "your tradition of freedom" which makes possible such creative political acts as the sit-in and the teach-in. The United States, he said, disposes of possibilities of good unmatched by any other country in the world.

If their view of the United States seemed at first improbable, then innocent and touching, the emotion the Vietnamese have for their own country seemed utterly alien, and even dangerous. But by the end of my visit I began to feel less estranged. Discovering the essential purity of their own patriotism showed me that such an emotion need not be identical with chauvinism. (How sensitive the Vietnamese are to the difference was clear in the only slightly concealed distaste of people I met in Hanoi for recent developments in China, like the cult of Mao and the cultural revolution.) If the Vietnamese could make such distinctions, so could I. Of course, I knew perfectly well why the attitude the Vietnamese expected of me was in fact so difficult. Ever since World War II, the rhetoric of patriotism in the United States has been in the hands of reactionaries and yahoos; by monopolizing it, they have succeeded in rendering the idea of loving America synonymous with bigotry, provincialism, and selfishness. But perhaps one shouldn't give up so easily. When the chairman of the Writers Union, Dang Thai Mai, said in his speech of welcome to Bob, Andy, and myself, "You are the very picture of the genuine American," why should I have slightly flinched? If what I feel is that flag-waving Legionnaires and Irish cops and small-town car salesmen who will vote for George Wallace are the genuine Americans, not I—which I fear part of me does feel—isn't that cowardly, shallow, and simply untrue? Why should I (we) not think of myself (ourselves) as a genuine American? With a little more purity of vision—but one would have to close the seepage of private despair into public grievances—maybe an intelligent American who cares for the other ninety-six percent of the human population and for the bio-ecological future of the planet could love America, too. Probably no serious radical movement has any future in America unless it can revalidate the tarnished idea of patriotism. One of my thoughts in the closing days of my stay in North Vietnam was that I would like to try.

Unfortunately, the first test of my vow came much sooner than I expected, almost immediately, in the first hours after leaving Hanoi the evening of May 17, and I failed right off. I wish something could be arranged to insure a proper "coming down" for visitors to North Vietnam in the first days after their departure. Unprepared, the ex-guest of the Democratic Republic of North Vietnam is in for a series of brutal assaults. Thirty minutes out of Hanoi, it was the spectacle of the drunken Polish members of the International Control Commission sitting around a table in the forward part of the plane dealing out a deck of pornographic playing cards. As we made our first touchdown, in the small airfield of Vientiane, it was seeing the landing area crowded with planes marked Air America (the C.I.A.'s private airline) which leave daily from here to drop napalm on villages in Northern Laos held by the Pathet Lao. Then came the taxi ride into Vientiane itself, River City U.S.A. (as Andy dubbed it), sordid outpost of the American empire. Servile, aggressive Laotian pedi-cab drivers trying to hustle a fare, an elderly lady tourist or a freaked-out hippie or an American soldier, weaved in and out of the Cadillacs driven by American businessmen and Laotian government personnel. We passed the movie theatres showing skin flicks for the GI's, the "American" bars, the strip joints, stores selling paperbacks and picture magazines that could have been transplanted directly from Times Square, the American Embassy, Air France, signs for the weekly meeting of the Rotary Club. In the lobby of the Lane Xang, the one "modern" hotel in Vientiane, we bought copies of *Newsweek* and *Time* to catch up on what had been going on, during our absence of two weeks, in our world. Minutes later, Bob, Andy, and I were sitting on benches covered with thick red plastic in the hotel's air-conditioned cocktail lounge, getting drunk, soaking up Muzak, and poring helplessly, incredulously, and eagerly through the magazines. We began cracking hysterical jokes, with Andy further amplifying on his running gag about the Lone Ranger and Tonto that had been Bob's and my delight since the beginning of the trip—only it wasn't funny now. We debated going out and buying some grass (what else could one do here?) but decided against it, mainly because we were reluctant to go into the street and get even more depressed. By midnight we were all feeling positively sick.

When dawn came four insomniac hours later, I could see out the window of my room across the flat, almost dry Mekong River. The river bed is an unguarded frontier, for what lies on the far side is Thailand, another, much more important American colony, home of the bases from which most planes take off daily to bomb the country we had just left. . . . And so on, out and out, further away from North Vietnam.

Due to one of the misadventures typical of the ICC flights, we had already spent four days in Vientiane before we went to Hanoi, staying at this very hotel, walking all over the town we'd just driven through. And though we had been jolted by its sordidness then, it seemed now that we couldn't have taken its full measure. And yet, of course, it had all been there before, and we'd seen it. In contrast to her subtler dealings with Western Europe, America exports to Southeast Asia only the most degraded aspects of her culture. And in that part of the world there is no dressing up or concealing the visible signs of American might. Though it could be helpful anyway to abstain from *Time* and *Newsweek* for at least ten days after a visit to North Vietnam, an American must brace himself for a big cultural shock—reverse cultural dislocation, I suppose—when the first environment he sees after leaving Hanoi is a place like Vientiane.

Remembering the intimations I'd had in North Vietnam of the possibility of loving my own country, I wanted very much not to react crudely, moralistically, not to slip back into the old posture of alienation. And after a while the keenest part of my outrage did subside. For the anger an

American is likely to direct toward the emblems of his country's imperial dominance isn't founded simply upon their inherent repulsiveness, which permits no reaction other than aversion, but rather upon the despairing conviction that American power in its present form and guided by its present purposes is *invincible*. But this may not be, probably isn't, the case. The Vietnamese, for one, don't think so. And their wilder judgments do, by this time, have a claim to be taken seriously. After all, who—except the Vietnamese themselves—would have predicted on February 7, 1965, that this small, poor nation could hold out against the awesome cruelty and thoroughness of American military force? But they have. Three years ago, enlightened world opinion pitied the Vietnamese, knowing that they couldn't possibly stand up to the United States; and the slogan of people protesting against the war was "Peace in Vietnam." Three years later, "Victory for Vietnam" is the only credible slogan. The Vietnamese don't want anybody's pity, as people in Hanoi told me; they want solidarity. The "tragedy" is Johnson's and the American government's, for continuing the war, Hoang Tung said. "There are many difficulties until the war ends," he added, "but we remain optimistic." For the Vietnamese, their victory is a "necessary fact."

The consequences for Vietnam of the eventual defeat of the American invasion are not hard to envisage. They will consist, for the most part, in unqualified improvements over the present situation: cessation of all bombing, withdrawal of American troops from the South, the collapse of the Thieu-Ky government, and the accession to power of a government dominated by the National Liberation Front, which some day, but not in the near future (according to the present leadership of the NLF), will unite with the Hanoi government so that at long last the divided country will be reunified. But one can only speculate about the consequences of this defeat for the United States. It could be a turning point in our national history, for good or bad. Or it could mean virtually nothing—just the liquidation of a bad investment that leaves the military-industrial establishment free for other adventures with more favorable odds. To believe that things in America could move either way doesn't seem to me overly optimistic. But then, if there's at least some hope for America, 1968 would be the wrong time for people in this country who look toward radical change to lose heart.

As Hegel said, the problem of history is the problem of consciousness. The interior journey I made during my recent stay in Hanoi made the truth of this grandiose maxim sharp and concrete for me. There, in North Vietnam, what was ostensibly a somewhat passive experience of historical education became, as I think now it had to, an active confrontation with the limits of my own thinking.

The Vietnam that, before my trip to Hanoi, I supposed myself imaginatively connected with, proved when I was there to have lacked reality. During these last years, Vietnam has been stationed inside my consciousness as a quintessential image of the suffering and heroism of "the weak." But it was really America "the strong" that obsessed me—the contours of American power, of American cruelty, of American self-righteousness. In order eventually to encounter what was there in Vietnam, I had to forget about America; even more ambitiously, to push against the boundaries of the overall Western sensibility from which my American one derives. But I always knew I hadn't made more than a brief, amateurish foray into the Vietnamese reality. And anything really serious I'd gotten from my trip would return me to my starting point: the dilemmas of being an American, an unaffiliated radical American, an American writer.

For in the end, of course, an American has no way of incorporating Vietnam into his consciousness. It can glow in the remote distance like a navigator's star, it can be the seat of geological tremors that make the political ground shake under our own feet. But the virtues of the Vietnamese are certainly not directly emulatable by Americans; they're even hard to describe plausibly. And the revolution that remains to be made in this country must be made in American terms, not those of an Asian peasant society. Radical Americans have profited from the war in Vietnam, profited from having a clear-cut moral issue on which to mobilize discontent and expose the camouflaged contradictions in the system. Beyond isolated private disenchantment or despair over America's betrayal of its ideals, Vietnam offered the key to a systematic criticism of America. In this scheme of use, Vietnam becomes an ideal Other. But such a status only makes Vietnam, already so alien culturally, even further removed from this country. Hence the task awaiting any sympathetic person who goes there: to understand what one is nevertheless barred from understanding. When American radicals visit North Vietnam, all things are thrown into question—their necessarily American attitudes to Communism, to revolution, to patriotism, to violence, to language, to courtesy, to eros, not to mention the more general Western features of their identity. I can testify that, at the very least, the world seems much bigger since I went to North Vietnam than it did before.

I came back from Hanoi considerably chastened. Life here looks both uglier and more promising. To describe what is promising, it's perhaps imprudent to invoke the promiscuous ideal of revolution. Still, it would be a mistake to underestimate the amount of diffuse yearning for radical change pulsing through this society. Increasing numbers of people do realize that we must have a more generous, more humane way of being with each other; and great, probably convulsive, social changes are needed to create these psychic changes. To prepare intelligently for radical change requires not only lucid and truthful social analysis: for instance, understanding better the realities of the distribution of political and economic power in the world which have secured for America its present hegemony. An equally relevant weapon is the analysis of psychic geography and history: for instance, getting more perspective on the human type that gradually became ascendant in the West from the time of the Reformation to the industrial revolution to modern post-industrial society. Almost everyone would agree that this isn't the only way human beings could have evolved, but very few people in Europe and America really, organically *believe* that there is any other way for a person to be or can *imagine* what they might be like. How can they when, after all, that's what they are, more or less? It's hard to step over one's own feet.

And yet, I think, the path isn't altogether blocked. Of course, most people are unlikely to come to a direct awareness of how local is the human type they embody, and even less likely to appreciate how arbitrary, drastically impoverished, and in urgent need of replacement it is. But they do know something else: that they are unhappy and that their lives are cramped and savorless and embittered. If that discontent isn't channeled off to be repaired by the kind of psycho-therapeutic awareness which robs it of social and political, of historical, dimension, the wide prevalence of unfocused unhappiness in modern Western culture could be the beginning of *real* knowledge—by which I mean the knowing that leads simultaneously to action and to self-transcendence, the knowing that would lead to a new version of human nature in this part of the world.

Ordinarily, changes in the human type (which is to say, in the quality of human relations) evolve very slowly, almost imperceptibly. Unfortunately, the exigencies of modern history being what they are, we can't be content to wait for the course of natural deliverance. There may not be enough time, given this society's strong taste for self-destructiveness. And even if Western man refrains from blowing himself up, his continuing as he is makes it so awfully hard, perhaps soon intolerably so, on the rest of the world—that is, most of the world, the more than two billion people who are neither white nor rich nor as expansionist as we are. Just possibly, the process of recasting the particular historical form of our human nature prevalent in Europe and America can be hurried a little, by more people becoming aware of capacities for sentiments and behavior that this culture's values have obscured and slandered.

An event that makes new feelings conscious is always the most important experience a person can have. These days, it's a pressing moral imperative as well. I was very lucky, I think: my ignorance, my empathic talents, and the habit of being dissatisfied with myself worked together to allow just such an experience by the end of my trip to North Vietnam in May. (Though the new feelings that were revealed to me are undoubtedly quite old in a historical sense, I personally had never experienced them before, or been able to name them, or been hitherto capable of believing in them.) Now, once again, I am far from Vietnam, trying to make these feelings live here in an appropriate and authentic form. That sounds difficult. Still, I doubt that what's required is a great effort of "holding on." In and by itself, such an experience is transformative. It is indelible.

I recognized a limited analogy to my present state in Paris in early July when, talking to acquaintances who had been on the barricades in May, I discovered they don't really accept the failure of their revolution. The reason for their lack of "realism," I think, is that they're still possessed by the new feelings revealed to them during those weeks—those precious weeks in which vast numbers of ordinarily suspicious, cynical urban people, workers and students, behaved with an unprecedented generosity and warmth and spontaneity toward each other. In a way, then, the young veterans of the barricades are right in not altogether acknowledging their defeat, in being unable fully to believe that things have returned to pre-May normality, if not worse. Actually it is they who are being realistic. Someone who has enjoyed new feelings of that kind—a reprieve, however brief, from the inhibitions on love and trust this society enforces—is never the same again. In him, the "revolution" has just started, and it continues. So I discover that what happened to me in North Vietnam did not end with my return to America, but is still going on.

JUNE–JULY 1968